PRAISE

OVERWHELMED BY GOD
AND NOT YOUR TROUBLES

In his latest book *Overwhelmed by God and Not Your Troubles*, Steve takes us where few would want to go—to the end of ourselves—to discover the overwhelming goodness and greatness of our God and His plans for our lives. Birthed from personal experiences and ongoing suffering that left him hanging by faith, waiting upon the Lord, Steve met God in a way only dying to oneself allows. It is a book filled with Bible stories in their context and applied to our everyday lives that will bring you to be overwhelmed by His grace and love and power and might. I highly recommend you sit and read and allow the Lord to *Overwhelm* you time and again (see Ps. 102:1).

Pastor Jack Abeelen
Senior Pastor, Morningstar Christian Chapel

Struggles and trials are commonplace, but throughout history, those who overcame did so because they adopted the right outlook toward the circumstances confronting them. In his new book, *Overwhelmed by God and Not Your Troubles*, Pastor Steve Mays helps us gain the correct viewpoint. For every individual who currently is, or has ever had to face discouragement and difficulties (and that includes all of us!), this book will produce the right perspective.

David Barton
Founder and President, WallBuilders

"Trust in the Lord with all your heart . . ." God tells us in Proverbs 3. Most Christians know this truth, but just *how* do we do it? What you have here in your hands is more than just another book to stash on some shelf. You'll be "overwhelmed" with the nuts-and-bolts, the tools on how to trust the God you serve. Like drinking from a divine fire hose, is this masterful use of the Word.

Charles H. Browning, Ph.D.
Marriage and Family Therapist, Foundation for Applied Biblical Counseling

As an architect, I've spent my life designing various types of buildings that fit my client's needs and desires. The common thread in my work is making sure that the foundation for each building, no matter the style, is strong, fortified and solid. Steve Mays is a spiritual architect—making sure that all whom he reaches out to stand strong on the solid foundation of God's Word. In *Overwhelmed by God and Not Your Troubles*, Steve reminds Christians that the overwhelming problems we face in life should not be our primary focus and concern, but instead we should turn to the foundation of our life—*God*—and allow ourselves to be overwhelmed by His goodness, love, mercy and grace. I believe this book is a must read for all of us who find ourselves overwhelmed with the problems and cares of this world.

John G. Cataldo, A.I.A., C.S.I.
Founder, Cataldo Architects, Inc.

I've known Pastor Steve Mays for many years, and if there is someone who understands God's heart and its bearing on our lives, it's him. We are all vulnerable to being overwhelmed by life's challenges, but an overcoming perspective and hope are clearly presented and prescribed in the pages that follow. The timing for this message couldn't be better and its messenger couldn't be more qualified to share it.

Pastor Bob Coy
Senior Pastor, Calvary Chapel Fort Lauderdale

Pastor Steve Mays helps us understand how to exchange being overwhelmed by trying circumstances, challenging trials, difficult news and bad days, with an "other-world" kind of overwhelming. He shows us that when God overwhelms us with who He is and what He does, the troubles that normally overwhelm us won't overwhelm us anymore. Read this book and be overwhelmed with God instead of your troubles and difficult circumstances!

Pastor Jay Dennis
Senior Pastor, First Baptist Church at the Mall, Lakeland

In a world without solid answers to difficult questions, without truth and substance in its perceptions, *Overwhelmed by God and Not Your Troubles* is a refreshing stream of godly wisdom. That's because its source is not just theory or theological correctness. It flows, I believe, from Steve's journey with the Lord through more surgeries than most of us will ever have visits to the dentist. Through personal heartache and long periods of convalescing, Steve has garnered the grace and sustaining strength of God and His Word and put it onto the page. Great job, my friend. I hope to take the correspondence course.

Pastor Joe Focht
Senior Pastor, Calvary Chapel of Philadelphia

Steve Mays's new book is a high priority for anyone who feels like they are drowning in a sea of anxiety because of the problems and circumstances they are facing in their life. Steve helps readers understand that if they allow God to overwhelm them with His attributes, His personality, His character and His promises, they will experience an attitude shift away from their problems and onto the Problem Solver—who will fill them with hope and peace.

Pastor Jim Garlow
Lead Pastor, Skyline Church, San Diego

A surfer gets caught in a set, goes over-the-falls and finds himself tumbling over and over in the riptide. Suddenly his world is nothing but turbulence, chaos and suffocating confusion. In times like that, the wise surfer will grab the leash that connects him to his board and follow it to the surface. For Christians, Scripture is the leash that puts our world into perspective and allows us to fill our lungs with fresh, clean air. In *Overwhelmed by God and Not Your Troubles*, my friend Steve Mays helps you "tie on the leash," so to speak, so you'll be able to find the right perspective when circumstances overtake you.

Pastor Greg Laurie
Senior Pastor, Harvest Christian Fellowship, Riverside

As Pastor Steve's son, I have personally witnessed my father struggle with his physical condition and understand how an individual in his situation could feel completely overwhelmed. However, his trust in and understanding of God's love allowed him to conquer these challenges and to provide a great example of how God can overwhelm the overwhelmed. Definitely a must read for anyone facing difficult times in their life or struggling to yield to the Spirit of God.

Nathan Mays
Proud Son

When an outstanding spiritual leader like Steve Mays writes with vulnerability about his own personal experience of God's grace and goodness in difficult times, it's a must read. Here is an on-time-for-our-times book for all who, at times, are underwhelmed by God's presence and power and as a result are overwhelmed by the perplexities and pressures of life.

Dr. Lloyd John Ogilvie
Bestselling Author and Former U.S. Senate Chaplain

Steve Mays is as close to a modern day apostle Paul as you can get. He has mentored a host of Timothys, and just like Paul, he is no stranger to troubles. Steve's teaching and experience are always clothed in Scripture, so if you are overwhelmed with troubles, read this book. Steve will show you how to refocus on what really counts!

Tom Pearce
National Director, Shepherding the Next Generation

Is it possible to stand strong against the seemingly endless trials that rage against us today? In *Overwhelmed By God and Not Your Troubles*, Pastor Steve Mays reminds us that God is our strong tower always and forever. Pastor Steve provides Scripture-driven applications to overcoming the sense of helplessness we often feel during the trials life brings us. Instead of fear we should look to God's power in our lives.

Tony Perkins
President, Family Research Council

Steve Mays doesn't follow the trend of many writers by choosing the trendy themes that skirt the most difficult problems in life. His personal experiences enable him to explore the human dilemma and conflicts in living. *Overwhelmed by God and Not Your Troubles* is relevant, practical and ideal for these times, when truth is downgraded and simple answers are not satisfying.

Ross S. Rhoads
Chaplain, Billy Graham Evangelistic Association

Steve Mays has written a must-read book. *Overwhelmed by God and Not Your Troubles* offers both hope and encouragement. We encourage you to read and reflect on what Steve has written.

Jay and Jordan Sekulow
Jay Sekulow, Chief Counsel, American Center for Law and Justice
Jordan Sekulow, Executive Director, American Center for Law and Justice

We've all been there . . . we've all felt like drowning when troubles swell around us like large waves. But in this new book, Steve Mays reminds us that our Savior not only stands above the turbulence, He is *in it*, He is God *with* us! So if you feel as though you are "going under," take time to plunge into the first chapter of *Overwhelmed by God and Not Your Troubles*—you'll find the focus you need, as well as the strong grip of Jesus to help you rise above the worst of storms.

Joni Eareckson Tada
Founder and CEO, Joni and Friends International Disability Center

OVERWHELMED by
GOD
and NOT YOUR TROUBLES

STEVE MAYS

Regal

For more information and
special offers from Regal Books, email us at
subscribe@regalbooks.com

Published by Regal
From Gospel Light
Ventura, California, U.S.A.
www.regalbooks.com
Printed in the U.S.A.

Published in association with the literary agency of FM Management,
34332 Port Lantern, Dana Point, CA 92629

Library of Congress Cataloging-in-Publication Data
Mays, Steve.
Overwhelmed by God and not your troubles / Steve Mays.
pages cm
ISBN 978-0-8307-6745-8 (trade paper)
1. God (Christianity)—Attributes. 2. Suffering—Religious aspects—Christianity. I. Title.
BT130.M43 2013
248.8'6—dc23
2013027539

Rights for publishing this book outside the U.S.A. or in non-English languages are administered by Gospel Light Worldwide, an international not-for-profit ministry. For additional information, please visit www.glww.org, email info@glww.org, or write to Gospel Light Worldwide, 1957 Eastman Avenue, Ventura, CA 93003, U.S.A. To order copies of this book and other Regal products in bulk quantities, please contact us at 1-800-446-7735.

I dedicate this book to Jeff Dorman, Jeff Gill and the Board of Directors at Calvary Chapel South Bay.

To Jeff Dorman, whom God has miraculously converted from Judaism to Christianity: I marvel at the mind God has given to you, and how you have used your skills as a lawyer to righteously guide our church and so many others with the conviction of the Holy Spirit and the passion of Jehovah our God.

To Jeff Gill, who has taught me more about serving and being joyful than anyone else I know: your love for God's Word and your passion to help and minister to God's people have made you the man you are today—a man of compassion, commitment and, most of all, a man of character. And for that, I bless the work of the Holy Spirit in your life.

To the Board of Calvary Chapel South Bay: what can I say, but thanks to each of you for your faithfulness all these years. You have allowed me the great privilege to teach God's Word to this dying world without compromises or excuses. But also, you have shared me unselfishly with other ministries in the Body of Christ that are hurting and looking for God's help. When they could not pay, you absorbed the cost for them, and for that, I honor each of you and simply say, "Thanks."

Contents

Acknowledgments

Thanks be unto our God for all He has done for me personally. When I was in the gutter ready to die, He had another plan for my life. This Christian walk has not been easy, but He has given me the strength and courage to go on and never quit. I am so amazed at how He has healed my mind and heart so that I am able to put down on paper the wonderful work He has done in me and for my family. I am eternally grateful for His mercy and kindness.

Thanks to you, the reader of this book. It's because of you and your encouragement of me that made it possible for you to hold this book in your hands. This book was written in the midst of suffering, pain and overwhelming circumstances in my life. God took all my complaining and turned it into rejoicing, and then God asked me one simple question in the hospital: "Stephen, why are you so overwhelmed?" The rest is history. Now I am overwhelmed by His goodness and His grace.

Thanks to my co-writer and National Ministry Outreach Director, Melinda Kay Ronn, who has, for the past ten years, not only helped me get my thoughts in print, but also helped me bring the Word of God to national leaders and ministries worldwide. I'm grateful for her tireless enthusiasm in helping me "kick it up a notch!"

Thanks to Kelly Click for her unending labor of reading and editing and rereading and reediting—even with a house full of kids. Thanks also to Kevin, her husband and my worship leader, who unselfishly allowed Kelly to accomplish all she had to do to make sure this book retained my heart in it.

Thanks to Tricia Bennett, my copyeditor, who has gone beyond what she normally does to make this a great read, and most of all for her honesty in challenging me to always think about the reader. She was always right.

Thanks to Steve Chin and his wife, Virginia, who gave of themselves and sacrificed vacation days to make sure we accomplished what needed to be done. I'm grateful for Steve's management skills and the labor he put into overseeing the project—which meant keeping me on a deadline, which is not an easy task! Thanks, Steve, for your vision, patience and the many hours you spent helping to make this book the best it could be.

Thanks to my staff at Calvary Chapel South Bay whose prayers sustained me, and whose words of encouragement inspired me to keep preaching the Word of God without compromise, and who enabled me to pursue such projects as this book. To Pastor Rob Stoffel, who stood in my place, ministering to the body of believers in my absence—thank you.

Thanks to all the staff at Regal Books, including Stan Jantz, who made the journey of writing this book a fruitful one. To Alexis Spencer-Byers, who had the task of editing my book: thank you so much for not removing my heart from the pages, but rather enhancing it and uniting it with the reader.

To a dear friend, Mark Ferjulian, who believes in me and wants to present me rightly in the publishing world, as well as in other ventures down the road: thanks so much.

Special thanks to my wife, Gail, for making all this possible through her prayers, love, counsel and gracious spirit. I could never have made it through the hospital or through recovery without you, sweetheart. I know you will enjoy this book because it means that you can read it rather than being at the hospital again.

Pastor Steve

Foreword

When I first met Steve Mays, I thought we might have some things in common. That was an understatement. We instantly bonded and found that we both had experienced some very hard, life-shattering events in our personal life journeys. So when he asked me to write the foreword for his book, *Overwhelmed by God and Not Your Troubles,* I was honored. And after I read his book, I *knew* I had to write this foreword.

You see, I too, have been overwhelmed.

Many of my overwhelming circumstances—the kind that rock you off balance and deplete your hope—happened during my childhood, a time when rosy cheeks, laughter and sweet innocence should have ruled the day. But that was not for me. My laughter was consumed by fear and, later, hatred toward my alcoholic father—a man I had longed to receive love and care from, but who instead heaped abuse on me, as well as on my siblings and my mother. And, if that was not enough to overwhelm me, I found my innocence stripped from me by a farmhand who sexually molested me for several years. I felt that the only person who cared about me was my mother. But, after years of physical abuse at the hands of my father, she just couldn't take it anymore. So one day, I woke up to find that my mother had left. Her plan was to have me go and live with her once she got a job and had settled in. But that never happened.

Oh yes, I know what it's like to be overwhelmed.

And so does Steve Mays.

As a young man, his innocence was stripped away from him as well—by a trusted teacher at school. Steve's life spiraled downward after that event, leading him into a vicious cycle of drug abuse and violence.

Yet God can take what seems like insurmountable, overwhelming circumstances and change them into something good—something useful for His kingdom. Only God can heal our broken hearts and give us the love that we all so very much desire. Only God can change our lives!

You see, God reached out to me in the midst of my overwhelming circumstances. In the same way, God reached out to Steve Mays in the midst of his overwhelming circumstances. I am confident, dear reader, that the Lord will reach out to you in the midst of your overwhelming circumstances as well.

God not only reaches out to us when we are overwhelmed, He wants us to be overwhelmed *by Him* instead of our troubles. That's what I love about this book. It conveys the truth that we need to turn from those things that are devastating and choose to be overwhelmed by God's character and His attributes.

Steve has had ongoing health problems for many, many years, enduring more surgeries and hospital stays than anyone I know. But it was right in the midst of his overwhelming circumstance that the Lord spoke to him and asked, "Steve, why are you overwhelmed by this? I want you to be overwhelmed by Me." Because of that precious message from the Lord, this book was born!

This book will speak truth to your heart: God loves you and His many attributes and promises are yours to cling to, to use and to rest upon!

Are you overwhelmed by financial problems? God wants you to realize that He is your Provider and wants you to be overwhelmed instead by His provision and care.

Are you overwhelmed by the rejection of someone close to you? God wants you to understand that His love for you is constant and never changing, no matter what you are experiencing. He will never leave you nor forsake you.

There are many times in life when we can find ourselves being overwhelmed. Steve Mays does a great job laying out these setbacks and showing us how God's character traits and attributes are sufficient to conquer each and every one of them. The reality is that

14

when we focus on God and choose to be overwhelmed by Him, our circumstances will diminish in their capacity to rule our emotions and our lives!

My prayer is that you will see that you are not alone on this journey called "life," and that the issues overwhelming you right now are not insurmountable. God *can* and *will* work in your circumstances to bring about His glory. Focus on the Lord. Let Him overwhelm you, and you will find the peace, comfort and confidence to know that He is at work in your life.

In Christ,
Josh McDowell

Introduction

Are You Overwhelmed?

Does life have you caught in a powerful or violent whirlpool right now?
Are you overwhelmed by financial issues?
Do the bills keep stacking up while your bank account remains empty?
Are you overwhelmed by your marriage or your kids?
Are you overwhelmed by your singleness and loneliness?
Are you overwhelmed by any number of difficult circumstances?
Do you feel like you are drowning in a sea of despair and
God seems nowhere to be found?

Trials. All of us face them. What do you do when a trial hits your life with a vengeance? How do you respond to bad news, to crises, or when difficult circumstances happen to you? As a pastor, I frequently hear about people's trials. I've also experienced numerous trials of my own, especially relating to my health. No matter how unique or individual our trials may seem, they really are the same as what people all over the world experience.

It's very easy to become overwhelmed—feeling weighted down, engulfed, even crushed. These feelings can change our attitudes and our moods to the point that they produce a detrimental effect on our relationships and move us to act in any number of illogical or inappropriate ways.

In society today, everyone seems overwhelmed, for a multitude of reasons. Our relationships are often tense, which makes for feelings of being overwhelmed emotionally. The economics of our day result in a pervading sense of being overwhelmed financially—unemployment or underemployment, bills stacking up with not enough money in the bank to pay them, and the list goes on. Personal problems—such as the battle to diet and get our weight down or to be healthy when, around every corner, we have something wrong with us physically—can also cause us to be overwhelmed. So what do we do? How can we *not* be overwhelmed with so much on our plates and so many negative things surrounding us?

In the book of Psalms, David talks about being overwhelmed. For a long period, he was running from Saul. He says in Psalm 55:5, "Fearfulness and trembling have come upon me, and horror has overwhelmed me." That's a pretty terrible way to feel. David knows he's running for his life. He senses that at any moment, he could die. Fear has gripped his heart, because Saul is right around the corner and there's no place for David to go. He has no friends, no food, and no sense of security. He's overwhelmed. Psalm 61:2, however, communicates a different emotional state: "From the end of the earth I will cry to You, when my heart is overwhelmed; lead me to the rock that is higher than I."

A believer today might demonstrate a similar shift in a prayer like this: *God, You have to lead me to that Rock. I've lost it. I can't seem to find it. I don't remember where it is. I know it's big. I know it's strong. I know Jesus is the answer, but, God, I'm struggling. Would You lead me back?*

A typical human solution is to say, "I'll find the rock, and I'll get up by myself." Yet therein lies the problem. You see, we are overwhelmed by everything that's going on in our lives, but we are also overwhelmed with not being able to do anything about it!

God's response to our situation is: "I'll lead you, and I'll pick you up."

Psalm 143:4 conveys the sense so many of us frequently have of feeling crushed: "Therefore my spirit is overwhelmed within me;

my heart within me is distressed." Being overwhelmed is a global phenomenon—not just something we experience here in our own country or community. People in all places and times have struggled with not knowing what to do—with not being able to control what's happening in the world around us. When we perceive things seemingly falling apart, we get overwhelmed.

Bottom line, we have to change our perspective. We have to go to God. It's okay to feel overwhelmed, but remaining in that state of mind solves nothing. Do you ever get tired of hearing people talk about the same problems day in and day out? Months go by, and they are still downcast, staying in the same place emotionally and mentally. That's not how God wants us to live.

As a result of my own trials—my own feelings of being overwhelmed by circumstances that have come my way—I've given a lot of thought to what the Lord wants us to do with, and how He desires us to respond to, these very palpable feelings of being overwhelmed. I have concluded that God wants us to shift our focus away from the issues that make us feel overwhelmed and instead *allow Him to overwhelm us with Himself!* If we are overwhelmed by God, we will not feel overwhelmed by the problems that exist in our lives.

When we begin to let God overwhelm us with His love, grace, power, Spirit, provision, and so on, we will see Him work in and through our lives in a tremendous way. I firmly believe that God's will is for us to become overwhelmed with His goodness and His grace instead of being overwhelmed with our problems and trials. When we switch our focus and perspective, a change occurs—a change so dramatic and so real that the pesky problems we were previously overwhelmed with pale in comparison to the peace, contentment and joy that we find in Christ.

So, read on, dear friend. Dive into each chapter and allow God to overwhelm you with His love . . .

19

His grace . . .
His forgiveness . . .
His mercy . . .
His purpose . . .
His power . . .
His holiness . . .
His Spirit . . .
His Word . . .
His provision . . .
His victory . . .
And His promises . . .

1

Overwhelmed by God's Love . . .

instead of rejection and fear

*The love of God toward you is like the Amazon River
flowing down to water a single daisy.*
F. B. MEYER

*The Lord has appeared of old to me, saying: "Yes, I have loved you with an
everlasting love; therefore with lovingkindness I have drawn you."*
JEREMIAH 31:3

During my recent eight-month journey of being in and out of hospitals and away from pastoring my church, laid up in pain with titanium rods in my back from L1 to T10, I realized that God wants me to be overwhelmed with *Him* and not with my pain or my problems. As we went through this severe trial, my wife, Gail, and I really grasped this fact and were overwhelmed by God's love for us. He not only held us together, but He also held the church together. God lovingly took care of the church while I was away, and He showed His love to my wife and me in more ways than I can even mention.

Are you feeling overwhelmed right now? Are you asking, "Where is God? Why has He abandoned me in the middle of my

STEVE MAYS

problems?" If so, I can tell you without any doubt that God has not abandoned you. He is right there with you—by your side in the midst of your problems. God was present when I was in my hospital room, repeatedly pushing the button on the remote to the nurses' station, hoping to get a little bit more medicine to kill the pain I was experiencing. Was it a tough time? Yes, it was a horrific time in my life, but God was right there. Having problems doesn't mean that God is not present. In the book of Hebrews, the author communicates an amazing promise of God: "Let your conduct be without covetousness; be content with such things as you have. For He Himself has said, 'I will never leave you nor forsake you'" (Heb. 13:5).

So often, we focus on our difficulties: "I can't believe my boss... I can't believe my spouse... I can't believe my children... I can't believe I'm so broke ...." The reality is that we can choose either to be overwhelmed by our problems or to be overwhelmed with God and His presence in our lives. Although difficult things happen to us, God's love always remains the same. In fact, His love is irreversible and unchangeable. God has held me together and kept me from going crazy; He has never left me. Yes, God has been faithful. I pray that you, too, can make these statements. If not, keep reading as we examine how to make these truths a reality.

God wants to do a sanctifying and growth-producing work in each of us, and He uses both small, irritating problems and immeasurably painful trials to bring about His will—His good path for each of us. God wants to give us His peace. He wants us to comprehend and experience His incredible love for us. The prophet Zephaniah says it best: "The Lord your God in your midst, the Mighty One, will save; He will rejoice over you with gladness, He will quiet you with His love, He will rejoice over you with singing" (Zeph. 3:17). God pours out His love on us and rejoices over us.

Looking for Love

For many of us, John 3:16 was one of the first Bible verses we ever heard or memorized: "For God so loved the world that He gave His only begotten Son, that whoever believes in Him should not perish but have everlasting life." In this verse, God communicates the depth of His love for people.

One of the most tragic things in our lives is that we really don't understand the love of God. Every human being, no matter their culture, background or age, has a desire to be loved. But we don't often experience the unconditional love we long for in our relationships with our families, friends or spouses. We feel as if we have to prove that we're worthy of someone else's love.

I remember vividly feeling this way about my dad when I was young. For example, I was excited to play in my first Little League game. My dad was in the stands and saw me hit three home runs and one triple, going 4 for 4. I was thrilled, yet to this day, I can still remember my dad telling me, "Stephen, if you would have paid attention and really looked at the ball, you could have had four home runs!" Although my dad thought he was simply pushing me to be great, in reality, he was saying that I missed the mark in his book, and it crushed my heart.

Have you ever heard one of those "you missed the mark" statements from a loved one? Even in the most encouraging families and marriages, people often fail when it comes to loving unconditionally; as a result, our insecurities grow. Many of us, instead of feeling loved and secure, feel rejected and fearful. Therefore, when it comes to understanding the love of God, we often transfer our insecurities from our human relationships over to our relationship with the Lord. If our human fathers never said they loved us, we might question whether God really loves us. If we couldn't get the attention of our earthly dads, we likely doubt whether we have our heavenly Father's attention. If we strove to get our parents' acceptance and love, we probably also strive to get approval from everyone else, including God. Too often, our relationships are plagued by insecurities instead of being bolstered by love.

Jesus Christ was motivated by love. He came down from glory, humbling Himself in willful obedience to the Father and giving up His rights and His authority so that He could save us. He wasn't afraid of losing these things, because He understood that everything and everyone, including Himself, belonged to God. We, on the other hand, are usually motivated by insecurity rather than love. We don't want to give up our rights or our authority because we are afraid that we may lose everything we have attained and built.

Let's illustrate this: Perhaps we finally have a cherished girlfriend or boyfriend. However, we are so worried about losing this important person in our lives that we become controlling, mistrusting and clingy, to the point of driving him or her away. Or say we finally get a job that we really want. Now that we have it, we feel compelled to do everything we can to protect it—so much so that we become territorial, offensive and unable to work with others. Well, we have now forced the owner's hand to fire us.

When we are motivated by insecurity, we can lose the very things we are trying to hold on to so tightly. But if we are motivated by love—if we are convinced in our hearts that God has given everything to us—then we trust all that we have to our Father in heaven. If we do not comprehend the love of God for us, and do not rest in our heavenly Father as a God who can be trusted, then we feel as if we have to do everything ourselves. We have to pull our own strings. We have to manipulate people and situations to get what we want or keep what we have.

Jesus' way of going about things was entirely the opposite. He was confident in who He was—He belonged to God, and He and the Father were one. So He was able to minister with truth, never questioning His identity or value. He was able to allow Judas to kiss

Him even as he betrayed Him. He could eat with the publicans and touch the Samaritan and the leper. He could be in the home of a tax collector and even speak to the demon-possessed. Jesus never feared what other people thought about Him. He wholly focused on His purpose: to open the eyes of the blind, to heal the sick and lame, to teach the poor, and to bring the good news to all who would hear it. Jesus came to love people, not to condemn them. In fact, Jesus Himself is love!

The description God gave us for unconditional love appears in 1 Corinthians 13:4-8: "Love suffers long and is kind; love does not envy; love does not parade itself, is not puffed up; does not behave rudely, does not seek its own, is not provoked, thinks no evil; does not rejoice in iniquity, but rejoices in the truth; bears all things, believes all things, hopes all things, endures all things. Love never fails." This unconditional love that God has for us is a foundation to rest in and to model our own love after.

Yet too often we doubt God's love for us, especially when we feel that He has taken something or withheld something from us. We get overwhelmed when we face trials or difficult problems, and we immediately question God's love. *After all*, the erroneous thinking goes, *if God loves me, why would He allow me to suffer? Why would He take something or someone from me?* In truth, what we need to understand is that God is always thinking about what is best for others—including, but not limited to, what is best for us.

Most of the time we humans, on the other hand, are thinking only about what is best for ourselves. When someone close to us is sick or dying, we want that person to hang around—to stay alive—because, selfishly, we don't want to be alone; whereas it's possible God wants to release that person and give him or her a brand-new body. Or perhaps we want that new high-paying job, but God says no because He knows that ultimately it would hurt our relationship with Him and with our families.

In addition to doubting God's love for us, one of the greatest problems we face in life is accepting love from someone else. Many married couples let their love die because one of the spouses was terribly hurt by the other at one time. A wall is built up, and the hurt spouse does not allow the other back into his or her heart. When people's feelings get hurt, their defense mechanisms kick in and their hearts become hard, making it very difficult to break through and rekindle love. Sometimes people are so insecure that they simply don't allow another person to get close enough to them to love them in the first place. Fear of someone seeing them for who they really are and then rejecting them causes people to shun those who only want to reach out to them in love.

But why do we have such a difficult time accepting God's love for us? After all, He has never hurt us or rejected us. Yet, all too often, we keep His love at a distance. I believe the answer lies in the fact that we do not trust Him; we are fearful of His will in our lives. Therefore, when God says, "I want you to go," we ask, "Where are You going to send me?" Isn't it amazing that we think we know what's best for us rather than God who created us?

Often it boils down to what we want to do versus what God wants us to do. He says, "I want you to go," and we answer, "If it's to Hawaii, sure, but if it's to Iraq, no way!" What we don't realize is that if God wants us to go to Iraq, it will be better than being in Hawaii because we are where God wants us—in the center of His will. In fact, the most frightening place we can ever be is outside the will of God. The Lord loves us and has a plan and a purpose for our lives; if Iraq is part of that plan, God is going to use us to turn the place upside down.

As we read in John 3:16, Jesus came into the world to love people and to save them from their sins and from themselves. He didn't worry about His life; He didn't hold on to it, but gave it away for others. Jesus said that He didn't give His life because someone told Him to; He did it because He wanted to.

Just as in our world today, so too there were people in Jesus' time who didn't want God's gift of love. The Bible says that these people loved darkness rather than the light. But for those who were needful of and desiring God's love, Jesus came and touched them. He didn't come to the rich, the famous, or the people who thought they had it all together. He came to the poor, the sinners, and those who were down and out. Jesus shared His offer of love with anyone who was willing to receive it, as we read in John 1:12: "But as many as received Him, to them He gave the right to become children of God, to those who believe in His name."

God's Unlimited Love

God wants to fill our hearts with His glorious, unconditional love. It's a love that knows no boundaries—a love with no limits. Romans 8:35-39 describes the depth of it:

> Who shall separate us from the love of Christ? Shall tribulation, or distress, or persecution, or famine, or nakedness, or peril, or sword? As it is written: "For Your sake we are killed all day long; we are accounted as sheep for the slaughter." Yet in all these things we are more than conquerors through Him who loved us. For I am persuaded that neither death nor life, nor angels nor principalities nor powers, nor things present nor things to come, nor height nor depth, nor any other created thing, shall be able to separate us from the love of God which is in Christ Jesus our Lord.

What can separate us from the love of God? Absolutely nothing. Unlike our human relationships, which can crumble or end over very petty things, God's love is a constant in our lives. It is something

27

we can count on regardless of the trials or problems we face. God loved us before the foundations of the world were formed, and He will love us after we leave this earth. God loves us when we are faithful, and He loves us when we are faithless.

Let me ask you something personal. That problem you are facing right now—the seemingly insurmountable obstacle that is causing you stress and tempting you to doubt—is it bigger than God's love for you? Is it able to separate you from the love of Jesus Christ? Of course it isn't. So I want you to think about why you are so overwhelmed by it. I assure you that God's love for you is far greater and more powerful than the trouble you are experiencing right now. God's love will guide you into His perfect will for your life. He will do what is best for you because He loves you.

What exactly does God's love encompass, and what does it do? Let's take a closer look at an explanation from the book of John, beginning with that very familiar verse:

> For God so loved the world that He gave His only begotten Son, that whoever believes in Him should not perish but have everlasting life. For God did not send His Son into the world to condemn the world, but that the world through Him might be saved.
>
> He who believes in Him is not condemned; but he who does not believe is condemned already, because he has not believed in the name of the only begotten Son of God. And this is the condemnation, that the light has come into the world, and men loved darkness rather than light, because their deeds were evil (John 3:16-19).

From this passage, let's draw a few principles about the love of God, what it encompasses, and what it does.

God's Love Encompasses the World

The passage begins: "For God so loved the world . . ." Christ didn't come just for the Jews; He came for the entire world. God's love reaches every race, every culture, every nation, every language, every religion, every denomination and every age—every single person. That's why people from all races can come to Christ. That's why young and old can receive salvation. That's why people who have committed adultery or fornication can come to Christ and be saved. That's why those who are in jail, even those who have committed murder, can be saved—if they reach out to Jesus, who is "the way, the truth, and the life" (John 14:6).

When Christ came, He saw a world in need—a world that was living under the curse of sin, and a world that was racked with pain, suffering and darkness. Jesus saw people who were arrogant and unkind, and He saw people who were abused and abandoned. The Lord came for each and every person, desiring that all would come to Him and be saved. He did that because He loves every person who walks the earth.

Do we have the same love for people that Jesus does? Not really. We are very selective as to whom we love. In fact, we sometimes have a difficult time just loving our families, friends or co-workers. We easily can get angry and bitter with people because they do things that we don't like or that irritate us. Our love is self-centered. We think we should have honor and respect from people—and if we don't get it, how common is it for us to cop an attitude and become rude and unkind? That's not what Christ did. In fact, Jesus went to people who were despised by the general public—people like the Samaritans, the lepers, the beggars, the tax collectors and the religious leaders. Jesus even ministered to the Romans, who were politically in charge during that period and were hated by the Jews and others for their oppression. Jesus also reached out to women and children, which was culturally incorrect in His time.

Jesus was on a mission to love people; as many as would come to Him, He would love and save. Today, He draws near to us and says, "I love you; I want to come into your life." But we make stipulations with words like, "Okay, You can come in, but I'm going to choose my own spouse . . . I'm going to choose my occupation . . . I'm going to choose where to go and what to do."

That's not the kind of love God is asking for, because unconditional love surrenders 100 percent. Jesus' love encompasses all people, no matter who they are or what they have done. The Lord left His glory in heaven to come down to earth to love people—the very people who would betray Him, spit on Him, turn their backs on Him, and even crucify Him. When He was on the cross, did Jesus lash back at the people who beat Him and did so many other wretched things to Him? No. Instead, He prayed for them and asked His heavenly Father to forgive them. That's the love of God. That's the kind of love the Lord wants us to have toward one another.

Remember the story of Jonah in the Bible? God's plan for Jonah was for him to go to Nineveh and warn the people there to repent and find God's salvation. But Jonah didn't want to go to Nineveh. Its residents, known as the Assyrians, had treated the Jews horribly. They had humiliated the Northern Kingdom, stripping people naked and dragging them through the desert for miles. Jonah wanted the Ninevites to be punished; God, however, intended to save them.

Jonah tried to run away from God and His will, but he ended up in the belly of a great fish for three days and nights. Finally, that great fish spit him up on the shore of Nineveh, but Jonah's heart toward the people had not changed. As Jonah warned them of God's impending judgment, the people started to repent and turn toward the Lord. Jonah, of course, was not happy about that, so the Lord went after Jonah. While Jonah sat on top of a hill, under the shade of a tree that he loved, God sent a worm to destroy the plant.

Because of this perceived indignity, Jonah developed an attitude with God.

The Lord then asked Jonah, "What's wrong?"

Jonah replied, "My tree is dead."

God said, "Why do you love this tree more than you love these people?"

Jonah answered, "I don't want them in heaven; they're horrible people. I knew that Your great compassion would save them, and that's why I didn't want to come to Nineveh!"

The story of Jonah is not only about a nation that repented, but also about a man who was absolutely bent on being angry and unforgiving toward a group of people. God can use us for His purposes, even when we are filled with anger and bitterness toward other people, but He doesn't want to. He doesn't want us picking and choosing whom we are going to love. He wants us to have compassion toward everyone, not just those in our own little group—our own denomination, our own race, our own language, and so forth.

Here's a true story about an incredible Englishman, Henry Moorhouse. Before coming to know Christ, Moorhouse was a drunkard and a fighter. One day after Moorhouse's salvation, when Dwight L. Moody was in England leading a great revival, Moorhouse came to Moody and said, "You know, if I'm ever in the States, I'd like to preach in your church."

Moody, without thinking, said, "Well, you know, if you ever come over, I'll let you have the pulpit." Moody thought that the man would never come to the United States.

About two months later, Moorhouse called and said, "Hi! I'm in town. I'd like to go ahead and take you up on your offer to teach from your pulpit."

Moody, who was on his way out of town for a speaking engagement, didn't know what to do. He had never heard the man preach. Although concerned, Moody felt he had to let Moorhouse speak because he had told him in England that he could have his pulpit to preach. So while Moody was out doing his evangelistic crusade, Moorhouse preached from the pulpit to a packed crowd. Each night that Moorhouse preached, the church was completely full—standing room only.

Moody telegraphed his wife and asked, "What has been going on?"

She answered and said, "Don't even come back."

So Moody asked, "What are you talking about?"

She answered again, "Don't even come back, because he is preaching the love of God—something you don't preach."

Upset by what his wife had told him, Moody came back to his church to hear for himself what Moorhouse was preaching. With a critical and judgmental attitude, Moody listened to Moorhouse—and the message broke his heart and changed his life. Moody put a sign over his pulpit that read: The Love of God. Ultimately, Moorhouse's message revolutionized Moody's ministry.

Jesus Christ came to redeem mankind. But here we are, as Christians, too often putting people down, getting angry with them, and being selective about whom we love. That's not what God wants us to do. He wants us to be so filled with His love that we impart that love to others—no matter who they are. Our pulpit is the world.

That being the case, we need to have a heart for God that translates to others—the laundryman, our relatives, our neighbors, our leaders and everyone else God brings our way. When we see people, we shouldn't see culture, race, status or anything else, but people needing the love of God. Our message should be, "What can I do to help you get closer to God?" There's no room for bitterness, no room for resentment and no room for having an attitude. The only way people are ever going to come to understand the love of God is by the love that we show them. So instead of letting people and their problems overwhelm us, we need to allow God's love to overwhelm us and, in turn, share it with those around us.

God's Love Is a Gift

John 3:16 tells us that God "gave His only begotten Son" to us. In other words, God's love is a gift, freely given to us. This gift can only come from God Himself.

There's a horrifying yet powerful little story I have heard regarding a drawbridge operator and his young son. One day, the son begged his dad to take him to work. The child loved to watch the bridge go up and down so that the boats could pass through on the river. The dad turned to his boy and said, "You may come, but you need to stand by my side at all times. Son, are you listening? You must not leave my side."

While the dad was monitoring the bridge (which was open at the time), he told his son that a train was approaching, so he would have to bring the bridge down. But his son didn't answer him. Horrified, the dad started to panic, calling out to his son over and over again. Then he noticed his son, who had climbed out onto the bridge's gearbox. The dad looked at the oncoming train and back at his son. There was not enough time to run and get the boy off the gearbox before the train reached the river. Although he desperately wanted to save his son, the dad knew that he couldn't sacrifice the lives of all the people on the train. So, with tears in his eyes, he brought down the bar that lowered the bridge to allow the train to cross. As the tears flowed down his face, the dad noticed the people on the train, all waving and blowing him kisses as they went by, completely unaware that the man's only son had just died so that they could live.

On our own, even doing our very best, we would never be able to conquer sin and meet God's requirement for perfection. We just can't do it. God knows this. We were born sinners and do not have the power or the ability to conquer sin on our own. So God had to intervene. He chose to solve the problem by bridging the gap Himself. Only His Son, who was sinless, could take the punishment and penalty of sin for each of us so that we could be made righteous in God's eyes. Jesus willingly came to earth and took the penalty for our sins, even dying on a cross, so that you and I could have a right relationship with God and receive eternal life. Jesus said that He would lay down His life for the sheep, and He did so willingly because He loved us. God willingly gave His Son, who was blameless, as a sacrifice so that we could be saved. That is the love of God. That is the gift that He gives to all who choose to receive it.

God's love has no boundaries; its dimensions are limitless. Ephesians 3:14-19 relates its vastness:

> For this reason I bow my knees to the Father of our Lord Jesus Christ, from whom the whole family in heaven and earth is named, that He would grant you, according to the riches of His glory, to be strengthened with might through His Spirit in the inner man, that Christ may dwell in your hearts through faith; that you, being rooted and grounded in love, may be able to comprehend with all the saints what is the width and length and depth and height—to know the love of Christ which passes knowledge; that you may be filled with all the fullness of God.

Our human minds can grasp and visualize the width and height of something that can be seen tangibly, but we don't really have the capacity to grasp the depth of God's love. His love is so deep that we are never going to use up His grace—never going to use up all His forgiveness in our lives. Even though we are saved, I am convinced that many believers do not allow the depth of God's love to penetrate our hearts and lives. The Lord wants us to have depth in our faith—a depth that overflows with love, humility, patience and gentleness. It's a wonderful way to live when we are filled to overflowing with God's love, because then we see others the way

God sees them. We love people the way God loves us. When we possess that depth of faith, it changes us, our spouse, our kids, our friends, our community and the world.

Accepting God's Love Is a Choice

Unbelievably, God gives us a choice about whether to accept His love. Honestly, if I were God, I would make everyone as puppets. I wouldn't trust people to make the right decisions. I would *make* them love me! But God doesn't do that—He gives us free will; He lets us make our own choices. Because we are made in the image of God, we have the ability to think and choose. God wants us to freely love Him, just as He freely loves us.

It's not just that God loves us; He *looks* for ways to love us. We don't realize that, do we? We think things like: *God, I hope You're not mad, I hope You're not angry, and I hope You don't hurt me!* But God loves us unconditionally. He loves us just as we are. He understands our pain and our anguish. God knows that we do the best we can, but it's not good enough. He made us, after all: "For He knows our frame; He remembers that we are dust" (Ps. 103:14). So He sent His Son to be our strength, to be our sacrifice, and to help us in all our ways. The Lord sent His Spirit to help us make this choice. It's the biggest decision we will ever make—to choose to accept God's free gift of love through His Son and to follow Him.

God's Love Is Life

Finally, God's love is life itself—not only everlasting life in heaven, but also abundant life here on earth. Before I came to Christ, my life consisted of drugs, alcohol, violence and despair. But God grabbed me and showed me His love while I was still a sinner. His love gave me not only salvation and a home in heaven, but also a life worth living here on earth.

As believers, we have God's love, guidance, help, strength, gifts and Spirit to live our lives with true meaning and purpose. God uses us to reach people and change our world. What a glorious life He has given us! There will be problems—many problems, in fact—but God has also promised us a future home where there is no sickness, pain or death. In that eternal home, we will finally live a life free from sin. But even now—even in the midst of our overwhelming circumstances—we have life in Him, and it's a life worth living.

You might be thinking, *Pastor Steve, that all sounds great, but you really don't understand the difficult problems I am facing in my life right now.* Listen, friend, difficult circumstances will be part of every season that we walk through in life. No doubt, unfair events will occur or be inflicted upon us. It is when we encounter these situations that we become overwhelmed. We don't understand why they are happening, and we focus on questions like: *Why me? Why is this happening to me?* We should be focusing on what God is doing in the midst of our problems. Instead, we get angry, depressed or mean—and sometimes we even shake our fists at God.

Getting our eyes off the problems and choosing to see God working in the midst of the trials is the path we need to take. All of our overwhelming situations must be filtered through the truth of God's love. When we truly believe the amazing fact that God loves us, we can choose to be overwhelmed by God and His love instead of by our problems.

How can we choose to be overwhelmed by God? The answer lies in trusting Him completely and letting go of all other options. It is all about perspective. We can beg to be rescued from our trial, constantly surveying the options and striving to work things out to our advantage and comfort, or we can "cut the rope." That is, we cut the rope of the lifeboat that is clinging to the sinking ship and let the Lord, who has only good thoughts toward us, carry us away from the shipwreck of our lives. It is in the realization that the only good and true option is to trust in the Lord that we become overwhelmed by His love for us.

When we are overwhelmed with the trials of life, it is critical to focus on God's love—to realize that His plan is already in motion and that He is using our difficult situation to bring about His glory. So often we want to be delivered *out* of our struggles instead of seeking His glory *in the midst of them*. When we adopt the perspective that even our worst trial can be an instrument for God's glory, then we can fasten our seatbelts and begin accepting the ride rather than looking for a way out. As we become overwhelmed by God's love—as we realize and trust that He is at work in our situations—our fears are replaced with His peace.

I know all about wanting to give up. I've had numerous problems with my health in my adult years. But during this past year, I experienced by far the worst health challenge I have ever faced. The problem was with my back. I actually had to return to the hospital for the same surgery four times over a span of eight months as a result of screws popping out and other bones cracking or breaking. The pain was nearly unbearable, and so was the discouragement. During this time, I battled both depression and anger because I felt so out of control over my own body. Many nights were filled with intense pain, and so often I would just ask God, "Why?"

Satan would taunt me with lies like, "God is not listening to you," or "God doesn't care about you," but I knew better. I knew God loved me. I knew in my heart that God had led me to a great doctor who was committed to helping me. I was confident that God would not abandon me, even though I was struggling to see what He was doing in my circumstances. My faith was tested tremendously, but I knew He had a plan and that if I could just grasp a godly perspective, I would be all right.

We should rest so fully in the unlimited, unchangeable love of God that we trust Him to work in His way and on His schedule. When we do that, we will begin to see just how much the Lord loves us, and we will find peace and rest in the midst of our storms.

STUDY QUESTIONS

1. Instead of being overwhelmed with rejection and fear, what does God want us to be overwhelmed with?
2. Why is it that we feel rejected and fearful?
3. Why do we doubt God's love for us, and why do we have a difficult time accepting His love?
4. What exactly does God's love encompass?

✂ PRAYER ✂

Lord, thank You for Your love for me. Thank You that it is unconditional, irreversible and a free gift I could never earn. Overwhelm me with Your love. Let me be so full of Your love that it overflows to everyone I meet. Help me to love even the difficult people You bring into my life. Help me to love even when it is inconvenient. I want to love like Jesus does. I want to love others the way You love me. Amen.

2

Overwhelmed by God's Grace . . .

instead of guilt and failure

*Grace is the good pleasure of God that inclines Him
to bestow benefits on the undeserving.*
A. W. TOZER

*For by grace you have been saved through faith, and that not of yourselves;
it is the gift of God, not of works, lest anyone should boast.*
EPHESIANS 2:8-9

Have you ever had a rough day? Are you having one right now? During this time in my life, all days seem to be rough. Perhaps you can identify with my pain, or maybe you are swallowed up in guilt—committing that same sin you had repented of only to find yourself ensnared in it again and again. Or maybe you feel overwhelmed with failure in your life. I have good news—no, I have *great* news for you today. We can be overwhelmed by guilt and failure, or we can be overwhelmed by God's grace. Grace (God's Riches At Christ's Expense) is God's gift to us. It is unmerited favor: giving to us what we do not deserve.

God sent His Son, Jesus Christ, to redeem us from our sins. It's impossible for us to cleanse ourselves from sin, so God had to do it for us. When Jesus died on the cross, He wiped away, with His precious blood, all the stain of our sinful nature and poured His grace over all of our transgressions. He paid the penalty for our sins so that we didn't have to, and He sealed our redemption with His resurrection, assuring us that we would be in heaven with Him at the end of this journey on earth. Jesus' self-sacrifice was definitely an expression of God's amazing love and tender grace, as the apostle Paul so aptly expressed:

> But God demonstrates His own love toward us, in that while we were still sinners, Christ died for us (Rom. 5:8).

Grace is a gift. We don't do anything to merit it. But like any gift, in order for it to become ours, it must be received. If we have received Christ as our Savior, we have received God's grace—and when that is true, instead of being overwhelmed by guilt and failure, we can choose to allow God to overwhelm us with His grace.

We are all sinners; we are all unworthy. Because of our fallen nature, we will continue to be that way. But by the grace of God, He is at work in our lives. As we yield to the Holy Spirit, we will progress in our faith and in our Christian walk.

Satan's goal and desire is to condemn each of us. But because we as believers have the person of Jesus Christ living in us, it is His job to keep us in His power. The apostle Paul confirmed, through the testimony of the Holy Spirit, that in every city he visited, "chains and tribulations" awaited him. Yet he continued by saying, "But none of these things move me; nor do I count my life dear to myself, so that I may finish my race with joy, and the ministry which I received from the Lord Jesus, to testify to the gospel of the grace of God" (Acts 20:23-24).

This verse is packed with truth and significance for us as well. When the grace of God covers us, nothing is going to move us—not a divorce, a teenager running away, a business going under, a car accident causing injury or death, or a church having a split. No, nothing is going to move us away from the grace of God. Just as it did for Paul, the grace of God will keep us steadfast in our Christian journey, even during times of trial, and will sustain us in our race and ministry—ultimately with the goal of testifying about His grace.

For His glory and as a testimony of His grace, God wants us to shine from the inside out. He created each of us according to His perfect plan and for His specific purposes, and He continues to mold us into His image on a daily basis. As Paul described in 1 Corinthians 15:10, God's grace toward us is not in vain: "But by the grace of God I am what I am, and His grace toward me was not in vain; but I labored more abundantly than they all, yet not I, but the grace of God which was with me." This abundant grace, at work in us and for us, serves a purpose and will continue to work in and through us until heaven becomes a reality.

You are a child of God—a son or a daughter of the Most High God—and you are the apple of His eye. Yes, you might be poor in this earthly life. Yes, you might get fired from your job. Yes, you might get divorced. *None* of that changes who you are in Christ—that is, your identity in Him. His grace covers all your failures, all your guilt, all your transgressions and all your tribulations. Difficult to humanly comprehend, this grace of God is powerful. As Paul writes to the Corinthians, "And God is able to make all grace abound toward you, that you, always having all sufficiency in all things, may have an abundance for every good work" (2 Cor. 9:8).

God's grace abounds toward us so that we have what we need to accomplish all the good works He plans for us; that's an exciting gift. This grace also takes into consideration our weaknesses; it is "sufficient" for us, as God's "strength is made perfect in weakness" (2 Cor. 12:9). Many of us feel like we are failing time and again. Mercifully, God's grace does not leave us in that place of failure.

41

Yes, we need to be in fellowship with the Lord. Yes, repentance is crucial. But it is God's grace that establishes us:

> But may the God of all grace, who called us to His eternal glory by Christ Jesus, after you have suffered a while, perfect, establish, strengthen, and settle you (1 Pet. 5:10).

In other words, God is going to perfect us—doing His work through grace. He is going to, once again, strengthen us with His power. He is going to establish us, and we are going to be strong. God certainly uses our failures. In fact, often they are stepping stones that bring us to the grace of God.

From "Bad" to Grace: Four Women Become an Integral Part of Christ's Genealogy

I am always amused to see the credence some people place on a dog's pedigree. If a dog doesn't have the perfect genealogy, it can't even enter a dog show. For most of us, our own genealogy doesn't cross our minds or enter our day-to-day thinking, although some do find it interesting to investigate their roots and see where their family line takes them back in history.

Lineage and genealogy are often mentioned in the Bible. There are two different types of genealogies: There is the royal genealogy, and there is the bloodline genealogy of man. The book of Matthew follows the lineage of Joseph, whereas the book of Luke follows the lineage of Mary. Both show a direct connection between Jesus and David, which is important because it was foretold in the Old Testament that the Messiah would come from the line of David. So in Matthew's account, Jesus inherited the throne through his adoptive father, Joseph, commencing with Abraham and then from King David's son Solomon following the legal line of the kings to Joseph. Luke's Gospel goes back to Adam through the bloodline of Mary. In this way Jesus fulfills the prophecy by being a blood descendant of David.

We would probably think that the lineage of the Messiah would be filled with nothing but pristine and honorable people, right? Wrong. Interestingly enough, God uses even the genealogy of Jesus Christ to show how the Lord identifies with sinful people. Yes, Jesus was completely God, but He was also completely human, except without sin. The Bible tells us that He was tempted in all ways just like we are, but did not sin (see Heb. 4:15). We should appreciate the fact that there are people in the genealogy of Christ who are just like us—fallible, sinful and full of failure. Even so, because of God's grace in their lives, they are a part of His family tree.

We are going to take a close look at four women in Christ's genealogy (see Matt. 1:1-17). At first glance, we might think these women are too "bad" to be in the line of Christ. After all, one acted as a harlot, another was a prostitute, another was a Moabite (from a nation cursed by God), and another was an adulteress. That's quite a group, right? Yet God, because of His marvelous, abundant grace, had no problem identifying with these four women.

This truth is the golden nugget we each should take away for our own lives today. Do we believe that God is willing to identify with us, no matter what sinfulness we persist in or how much we have failed? God, in His grace, will always reach out to us—because grace is a gift that He is committed to and that He will never retract. Yet commonly, instead of accepting this gift of grace, we live with guilt because we neglect to seek after this God who loves us and gave Himself for us. So, let's take a look at Tamar, Rahab, Ruth and Bathsheba.

Tamar: Wanting the Right Thing but Going About It the Wrong Way

In Genesis, chapter 38, we find an incredible story about a young woman named Tamar. She was married to one of the sons of Judah, who was one of the 12 sons of Jacob (the 12 tribes of Israel). Judah and his brothers had sold their half-brother Joseph into slavery because of their jealousy of him. After selling Joseph, Judah left his family, went to a foreign country, and married a Canaanite woman. He then had three sons.

One day, Judah decided to give one of those grown sons in marriage to a Canaanite woman by the name of Tamar. Unfortunately, this son was wicked in the Lord's sight—and the Lord put him to death. After a time of Tamar's grieving, Judah gave his second son in marriage to Tamar. Why? The law stipulated that when a husband died, the brother who was next in line would marry the wife of the deceased brother in order to carry on the older brother's lineage. The second son didn't like what had happened, so when he went to bed with Tamar, out of bitterness he spilled his seed on the ground. This action displeased the Lord, and God killed him as well for his wickedness.

After all this, Judah did not want to give Tamar his third son, thinking there was a chance he might die as well. Notice that it was Judah who was breaking the law at this point. He refused to obey the law instructing him to give his next son in marriage to Tamar. As a result, Tamar, wanting to obey God's law and continue the family name (lineage), decided to take matters into her own hands.

Tamar found out that Judah was taking a short journey to cure the sheep and to sell them. So she removed her grieving garments, disguised herself by putting on the veil and clothes of a prostitute, and went to sit on the street and wait for Judah. When Judah passed by, he invited Tamar to come sleep with him. When it came time for payment, however, Judah didn't have any money. When Tamar demanded that he give her his staff and signet ring as payment, Judah gave in to the request of this woman he saw as a harlot.

A few months passed, and then Judah heard a rumor that Tamar was pregnant. He went berserk. He drew her out in front of everybody and accused her of playing a harlot. But Tamar produced the staff and signet ring that Judah had given her, and she let all the people know that these items belonged to her father-in-law, who was in fact the father of the child she was carrying.

Now, what is the lesson in this story? Tamar wanted the right thing, but she went about it the wrong way. God knew her heart and, in essence, communicates, "I love this woman. I don't condone or accept what she did, but her desire was to continue the line of Judah. So I'm going to put her in Jesus' genealogy, and through her, my Son will come."

Perhaps you can identify with Tamar. Maybe you want a good job, but you're going about getting it the wrong way. Being married may be a lifelong dream, but trying to make it happen in the wrong way is disastrous. Getting out of debt is a noble goal, but being deceptive to accomplish it is the wrong way. The end never justifies the means. Here, God's radical and abundant grace overflowed into Tamar's reality, because even though Tamar had disgraced herself, God's grace intervened, and she became a part of the lineage of the Messiah. Although Tamar took matters into her own hands (which was wrong), God chose to make her a part of Christ's genealogy because she had more righteousness than Judah did, as he forsook obedience to God's law.

Have you been jumping the gun? Have you been putting your foot in your mouth? Have you been trying to help God out? I challenge you to stop going after the right things in the wrong way. Let God's grace cover your mistakes and, instead of taking matters into your own hands, allow the Holy Spirit to bring about God's will in your life.

45

Rahab: Looking for a Way Out of Sin

Our second "bad girl" who found God's grace is Rahab. Her story is told in Joshua, chapter 2. Rahab was a prostitute in the city of Jericho and was a very wealthy woman. Even though she was a prostitute, Rahab had the knowledge of God in her heart. She had heard about this God who opened the Red Sea and who fed three million people with manna, and she understood that He was the true God. She believed that no one could stand against this God. Rahab was aware that judgment was coming. Her home was in the direct line of the army of Israel, and she was afraid.

When God brought two Israelite spies across her path, Rahab hid the spies from the leaders of Jericho, reporting falsely that they were not there at her house. Then, when the leaders of Jericho left her house empty-handed, she told the spies that she was aware of God's judgment over her city and asked them if they would save her and her family. The spies instructed her to hang a scarlet rag outside her window, promising her they would ensure that the Israelite army spared her home.

True to the spies' word, when Israel attacked the city of Jericho, Rahab and her family were protected and taken out of harm's way by the Israelite army. Rahab then left the life of prostitution and married an Israelite named Salmon; the couple ended up being the great-great-grandparents of David. Today we can read Rahab's name in the genealogy of Jesus Christ as written in the Gospel of Matthew. That's definitely God's grace at work! Rahab was a God-fearing woman even when she was working as a prostitute and living outside of the community of God's people. When it came time for her to choose sides, she sided with God and left her sinful life as a prostitute behind, having come to a personal faith in the Lord. Are we willing, as Rahab was, to leave our sinful lives behind and put our faith in Christ? If we are, then God will extend His grace to us also.

From the story of Rahab, we can gather that *God is not afraid to be identified* with a prostitute. So even if you're in some identity-labeling sin now, you can cry out to God and He will begin a work of trans-formation. He will give you an opportunity to repent of your sin and to choose everlasting life with Him. Then He will proceed to work miracles as you walk out your days on earth. Even if you are not sure of anything right now, ask God to reveal Himself to you. He will! You will hear Him, and He is going to reach out to you. He is faithful to do that.

Rahab refused to betray those spies. She refused to have any-thing more to do with Jericho, and because of that, God rewarded her. Not only is Rahab listed in Christ's genealogy, but she is also listed in the hall of faith in Hebrews, chapter 11, right along with Sarah—an incredible woman of God. By the way, Rahab ended up being the mother of Boaz, the man who married Ruth, our next highlighted "bad girl" touched by God's grace.

Ruth: A Stranger in a Strange Land Wanting to Fit In

Ruth was a Gentile, a Moabite woman, and her story is found in the Old Testament book of Ruth. Further back in Israelite history, the nation of Moab had been cursed by God because the Moabite people would not let Moses and the people of Israel cross through their country but instead forced them to go around. So the Bible was clear that the Moabites would be cursed and would never in-herit the kingdom of God.

Even so, God's grace was already at work in Ruth's story. An Israelite woman named Naomi, along with her husband and her two sons, left Bethlehem to escape a famine and went to Moab. They definitely should not have been dwelling in Moab, but their mistake became a trophy of God's grace. Ruth married one of Naomi's sons, and another young Moabite woman named Orpah married the other son.

After a while, Naomi's husband died. Ruth and Orpah helped take care of Naomi while managing their own families, but tragically, some years later, both Ruth's and Orpah's husbands (Naomi's sons) died as well. Naomi told the young women to go and find husbands in their own country because she was returning to Bethlehem. Orpah chose to stay in Moab, going back into idolatry, but Ruth chose to follow Naomi, telling her, "Entreat me not to leave you, or to turn back from following after you; for wherever you go, I will go; and wherever you lodge, I will lodge; your people shall be my people, and your God, my God" (Ruth 1:16).

Ruth was not concerned about her race or her culture. She had tasted that the Lord God was good, and she wanted to stay by Naomi's side, even though it meant leaving her own people, family and culture. It can be difficult to fit in when one is from a different culture and country, but in God, Ruth found a place to fit.

When Naomi and Ruth traveled back to Bethlehem, it was harvesttime. Ruth went to glean wheat in the fields, and as a result, she met Boaz, the man who would ultimately redeem her through marriage. Herein is seen a biblical principle: The moment we turn back to Him, no matter who we are or what we have done, God is going to show us grace and favor.

Although Ruth was from a country that had been cursed by God, she herself was redeemed—by one of the richest men in the city—because she chose to follow God instead of her culture. Maybe you don't feel like you fit in with the people you are hanging out with. Maybe you don't feel comfortable doing what your friends do anymore. Instead of blaming God for your circumstances, allow Him to overwhelm you with His grace, and choose Him over your nationality, race, creed, friends or culture.

Bathsheba: Hiding Her Sins but Needing Forgiveness

We will look at one final "bad girl" of the Old Testament who was touched by God's grace. Her name is Bathsheba, and her story can be found in 2 Samuel, chapter 11.

Bathsheba was the wife of Uriah the Hittite. Uriah was a soldier in King David's army, and at the time in question, he was out in battle. King David, who had come back from war—something he should not have done, by the way—was walking on the rooftop of his palace one evening and noticed Bathsheba taking a bath at her home nearby. The Bible tells us that Bathsheba was a very beautiful woman. It is obvious that David did more than just glance at this woman—his second mistake. The king then told his staff that he wanted Bathsheba brought to him. The text of Scripture doesn't specifically state as much, but no doubt they tried to talk him out of it. However, David insisted that he have Bathsheba, and he committed adultery with Uriah's wife.

Bathsheba ended up pregnant, and David tried to conceal his sin by calling Uriah home from the battle in hopes that he would sleep with his wife. But Uriah, being an honorable man, did not sleep with his wife, because he did not want to enjoy pleasure while his fellow soldiers were on the front line, fighting for Israel. As the next attempt in his cover-up, David wrote a note to Joab, the head commander in his army. In this note, King David clearly spelled out his murderous plans: "Set Uriah in the forefront of the hottest battle, and retreat from him, that he may be struck down and die" (2 Sam. 11:15).

So indeed Uriah died, and David took Bathsheba as his wife. Ultimately, one of God's consequences was that the baby Bathsheba bore became ill and died.

Let us reflect for a moment on how David's sin snowballed and eventually affected other people—as sin almost always does. David started the whole tangled mess by not being where he was supposed to be; he should have been on the battlefield rather than in leisure at home. He then allowed himself more than just a passing glance at Bathsheba.

Furthermore, the sin of adultery that David and Bathsheba committed did not solely affect them. David's great counselor, Ahithophel, was betrayed, and there would be future consequences for this man as a result. Joab was brought into the mix and was ordered to assassinate Uriah. Uriah, a faithful husband and valued soldier in David's army, was murdered. Nathan, a prophet of God, was lied to by David. God eventually revealed the truth of David's sin to Nathan, who boldly confronted the king with what he had done by telling David a parable that was specifically directed at him. Finally, the infant child of David and Bathsheba became ill and died.

In God's abundant grace, good did come from this awful situation. After being confronted by Nathan the prophet, David humbly confessed his sin and repented before God, who forgave and restored him. Nathan said to David, "The Lord also has put away your sin; you shall not die" (2 Sam. 12:13). What about Bathsheba? After all, because of David, her husband was murdered, her grandfather Ahithophel eventually committed suicide, her unborn baby died, and her reputation was disgraced. Through all of this, however, Bathsheba turned to God and brought forth a son named Solomon, who would end up being the next king of Israel and the one who would build the temple of God. Once again, God's grace prevailed, and Bathsheba's name is found written in the genealogy of Jesus Christ.

The Grace of an Amazing God

These four women are all found in the genealogy of Christ solely because of the grace of an amazing God who calls, loves, accepts and forgives sinners. Maybe you are like Tamar—wanting the right thing, but accomplishing it the wrong way and now feeling like God has rejected you. God sees your heart. He will never reject you. Or maybe you are like Rahab—being caught in your sin and looking for a way out. God will show you a way out through Christ. Or maybe you are like Ruth—seeming not to fit in. But you have a friend closer than a brother: Jesus. Or maybe you are like Bathsheba—hiding your sins and needing a God who will forgive you. Well, that's the God you have—He's more than willing to forgive you. The experiences of these four women powerfully illustrate that God put His hand on them and said, "I identify with you."

Through His immeasurable grace, God is willing to identify with each of us today as well. I know this full well, as I have been a recipient of God's unending grace. During one of my hospital stays a couple of months ago, I was not the most pleasant patient. I was angry at God and frustrated with my body, and I hate to admit that I vented my frustration on some of the nurses. I too fall down in sin, again and again. We all do. But with God's grace, and through repentance and forgiveness, we can get back up again. I once again cried out to God, and He faithfully picked me up and placed my feet upon the Rock of Jesus Christ. I repented, apologized, and let the Holy Spirit change my attitude by giving me God's perspective. His grace is truly sufficient and never-ending.

STUDY QUESTIONS

1. What four women are found in the genealogy of Christ, and why is it surprising that God included them in Jesus' family tree?
2. Why did God choose to include Tamar in Christ's genealogy?
3. Why did God choose to include Rahab in Christ's genealogy?
4. Why did God choose to include Ruth in Christ's genealogy?
5. Why did God choose to include Bathsheba in Christ's genealogy?

∽ PRAYER ∽

Lord, thank You for Your grace in my life. Thank You that You pick me up again and again. You never leave me alone nor withhold any good thing from me. You want me to follow hard after You; it is Your desire that my heart would mirror Yours. Thank You for never giving up on me, even when I am lost in sin. Even then, You orchestrate circumstances and trials that draw me near to You. Thank You that You alone can make my life a trophy of Your grace. You are willing to get Your hands dirty and reach down to hurting and lost people. Work in my brokenness, I pray, helping me to see and experience Your hands all over my life. Thank You for Your grace that never lets me go. Amen.

3

Overwhelmed by God's Forgiveness . . .

instead of bitterness and resentment

There are two ways of covering our sins: man's way and God's way.
If you seek to hide them, they will have a resurrection sometime;
but if you let the Lord cover them, neither the devil nor man
will ever be able to find them again.

D. L. MOODY

As far as the east is from the west,
So far has He removed our transgressions from us.

PSALM 103:12

Most of our problems, especially relational ones, stem from the issue of unforgiveness. We harbor resentment. We won't let go of our hurts or the misdeeds that people have committed against us. When our hearts are so full of bitterness, we don't experience the blessings of God. The Bible says, "For if you forgive other people when they sin against you, your heavenly Father will also forgive you. But if you do not forgive others their sins, your Father will not forgive your sins" (Matt. 6:14-15).

STEVE MAYS

God is not pleased when we harbor an attitude of bitterness, resentment or judgment. An unforgiving heart runs contrary to the very nature of God. Does God hold back His forgiveness when we sin or do something stupid? Does God tear us down when we mess up? No. God forgives us, takes care of us, and builds us up. If we are to be like Christ—if we have His life in us—then we are called to be an extension of who He is: forgiving, loving, gracious, merciful and kind. People are often turned off by professing Christians who do not reflect God's character in these ways. Bottom line, if a person is overwhelmed by bitterness and resentment, he or she needs to forgive; the best way to do that is to be overwhelmed by God's forgiveness.

Christ: Our Example of Forgiveness

Sometimes we say we forgive people, but we still feel that they have some type of deserved punishment coming to them. What a gift to us that Jesus never treats His children that way. Jesus freely, lovingly and unconditionally forgives. The Scriptures contain multiple illustrations of this truth. For example, when Jesus healed the paralytic, He said to him, with no qualifications, "Son, be of good cheer; your sins are forgiven" (Matt. 9:2). And when Peter denied the Lord, Jesus didn't say, "I told you so!" He had, in essence, communicated to Peter, "You're going to be hassled. Satan is going to mess with you, but I have prayed for you, and when you get done messing up, go strengthen your brothers" (see Luke 22:32).

When Jesus was on the cross, He said, "Father, forgive them, for they do not know what they do" (Luke 23:34). It's downright amazing that there was no resentment or bitterness in Jesus' statement, and no anger in His heart—just love—as He was being murdered on the cross. Jesus is our role model when it comes to forgiving people—no anger, no bitterness or resentment, and no sarcastic remarks. He just loved them.

Jesus' love and forgiveness know no boundaries. On one occasion, He opened up to a Roman centurion, a Gentile, who had asked Jesus to heal one of his servants. Even though the Romans were hated by the Jews at the time, Jesus accepted this "enemy" and healed his servant. God's forgiveness extends to every race, every culture, every country and every walk of life. I'm reminded of the thief who hung on the cross next to Jesus. In our human nature, we would probably think, *Well, he did something wrong; he deserved to be there.* But Jesus didn't think or communicate that. Rather, when the thief asked Jesus to remember him, Jesus kindly and graciously said, "Today you will be with Me in Paradise" (Luke 23:43). Truly, we humans would leave the thief on the cross, but Jesus wouldn't— and didn't—do that. In fact, the Bible says very clearly that God's thoughts for you are not of evil but for peace, to give you a future and a hope (see Jer. 29:11).

Throughout His time on earth, Jesus loved people and forgave them their sins. Whether it was lepers, demon-possessed people, adulterers, tax collectors, fishermen, the lame or those in high positions—He forgave them all. There are no boundaries on God's forgiveness. So no matter where we look in the Bible, our God is always forgiving, reaching out, and moving in the hearts of His people.

We are told in Isaiah 53:6 that "all we like sheep have gone astray; we have turned, every one, to his own way," yet in beautiful forgiveness, our iniquities have been taken away, because "the Lord has laid on [Jesus] the iniquity of us all." God doesn't just bury our sins; He gets rid of them. How? By laying them on Jesus.

Isaiah 43:25 says that the Lord "blots out your transgressions," and Psalm 85:2 tells us, "You [God] have forgiven the iniquity of Your people; You have covered all their sin." What amazing truths! We have a God who covers our sins—He isn't willing to expose us.

When we forgive people, however, what do we do? We bring up what they did again and again, especially when we are mad. We don't bury the sins; we remember them. We say we have forgiven those who have wronged us, but then we tell others all about what they did to us. We expose their sins time and again. Filled with bitterness, we refuse to even look at the people we supposedly forgave.

Bottom line, we have a God—modeled in Christ—who has completely forgiven us of our sins. He has buried them, washed them away, covered them and thrown them into the deepest sea. We are called to forgive others just as Christ has forgiven us. Moreover, the more we really allow ourselves to be overwhelmed by God's forgiveness of our sins, the more we will forgive others in the same way.

Forgiveness
Powerfully Transforms Lives

The Bible contains many incredible stories of forgiveness; one of them is found in the final chapter of the book of Jeremiah. This chapter details the fall of Jerusalem; in its final verses, it describes an incredible episode from the life of King Jehoiachin, who was the second-to-last king of Judah. Previously, when King Nebuchadnezzar of Babylon annihilated Jerusalem, he took many of Israel's prophets and spiritual leaders captive, including King Jehoiachin. Nebuchadnezzar put Jehoiachin in prison, and he stayed there for 37 years.

During this time, Nebuchadnezzar walked out among his kingdom and asked, "Is not this great Babylon, that I have built for a royal dwelling by my mighty power and for the honor of my majesty?" (Dan. 4:30). While the words were yet in his mouth, God drove him out of the kingdom and gave him the mind and heart of a beast. This mighty king, humbled by God, spent seven subsequent years living as a beast of the field. Nebuchadnezzar's son, Evil-Merodach, took over the kingdom's rule.

At the end of seven years, Nebuchadnezzar lifted his hands and began to praise the Most High God. He came back to the throne and upon discovering the horrible things his son had done in his absence, Nebuchadnezzar, in his anger, threw him into prison. Just a few years later, however, Nebuchadnezzar died, and once again Evil-Merodach was made king over Babylon. This is where our story of incredible forgiveness begins.

Jeremiah 52:31-34 lays out the facts:

> Now it came to pass in the thirty-seventh year of the captivity of Jehoiachin king of Judah, in the twelfth month, on the twenty-fifth day of the month, that Evil-Merodach king of Babylon, in the first year of his reign, lifted up the head of Jehoiachin king of Judah and brought him out of prison. And he spoke kindly to him and gave him a more prominent seat than those of the kings who were with him in Babylon. So Jehoiachin changed from his prison garments, and he ate bread regularly before the king all the days of his life. And as for his provisions, there was a regular ration given him by the king of Babylon, a portion for each day until the day of his death, all the days of his life.

So, right off the bat, the new king of Babylon pulled King Jehoiachin out of prison and gave him a kingship higher than all the ones in the Babylonian kingdom. What? Imagine rotting away in prison for 37 years and then instantly being given a kingdom again. That's what happened to King Jehoiachin. I have to wonder if Jehoiachin felt a little out of his element when he was freed. He had been king of Judah, yes, but he had spent the last 37 years in a prison cell. Is it logical to think he just picked up where he left off?

As a pastor, I have found that some people get used to their captivity. I am not just referring to an actual jail sentence, obviously. I have counseled many people over the years who, although they were saved, were not enjoying the freedom that Christ gave them at salvation. They had become used to their captivity. They were comfortable with their bad attitudes, their bitterness and their resentment. They were used to their criticism and selfishness. Sadly, some people would rather stay in their captivity or their feelings of being overwhelmed than enjoy the freedom of Christ and all that He has to offer.

What about you? Do you want to stay where you are? Are you going to remain inside the dark prison instead of being used by God? Are you going to be miserable for the rest of your days, protecting yourself from getting hurt again instead of reaching out and being a blessing to others?

Remaining in captivity is not what Christianity is about. Christianity is about newness and forgiveness. If we can't forgive, we can't move on.

Speaking personally, I had to forgive the man who molested me when I was in junior high. There was also the guy who shot me—I had to forgive and move on. Today, no matter what occurs in my life, I have to accept it and move on. Holding on to bitterness will destroy my ministry, destroy my marriage and destroy the message that God has given me to share.

So here in this small yet powerful story from the Scriptures, we observe a king of Babylon (not even one of God's people) showing more forgiveness than most of us give to others. In this story of Jehoiachin, we will examine six important lessons that demonstrate a picture of God's actions of forgiveness toward us.

Jehoiachin Was Brought Out of Prison by the King

Let's go back to the beginning of the story: "Now it came to pass in the thirty-seventh year of the captivity of Jehoiachin king of Judah, in the twelfth month, on the twenty-fifth day of the month, that Evil-Merodach king of Babylon, in the first year of his reign, lifted up the head of Jehoiachin king of Judah and brought him out of prison" (Jer. 52:31).

What strikes me most about this verse is that it was the king himself who led Jehoiachin out of captivity. The king of Babylon didn't send a servant or a soldier to set Jehoiachin free, which is what we would naturally expect; instead, he chose to do it himself. Imagine sitting in prison, with no hope of release, when all of a sudden the president of the United States shows up at your cell, unlocks the door, and says, "Come with me. I'm setting you free!"

The beauty of this story is that it parallels what God has done for us. The Creator of the universe—the God who made you and me—has Himself forgiven us and set us free. That's just how special we each are to God. He loves us so much that He has taken our sins upon Himself and set us free. We are forgiven by God Himself. Think about that for a moment. All those rotten words said, nasty attitudes held and sinful actions taken have been buried, washed away, blotted out and covered by the God of the universe.

In the book of Romans, Paul shares how grateful he is that Jesus rescued him from sin and death, given his own wretchedness:

> For the good that I will to do, I do not do; but the evil I will not to do, that I practice. Now if I do what I will not to do, it is no longer I who do it, but sin that dwells in me.
>
> I find then a law, that evil is present with me, the one who wills to do good. For I delight in the law of God according to the inward man. But I see another law in my members, warring against the law of my mind, and bringing me into captivity to the law of sin which is in my members. O wretched man that I am! Who will deliver me from this body of death? I thank God—through Jesus Christ our Lord!
>
> So then, with the mind I myself serve the law of God, but with the flesh the law of sin (Rom. 7:19-25).

It's obvious in these verses how trapped Paul felt, even though he hadn't been imprisoned for 37 years, as Jehoiachin was. We also can feel trapped in our sin—who is going to set us free? Who is willing to come help us? The good-news answer: Jesus Christ. No matter how long you have been in captivity, and no matter what you have done, Jesus Christ will set you free.

Notice also in Jeremiah 52:31 that the king lifted up Jehoiachin's head. In other words, he encouraged him and lifted his spirit. No doubt Jehoiachin, having been in captivity for so long, was depressed and without hope. It was the king of Babylon himself who encouraged him and gave him hope. In the same way, God lifts up our heads and gives us hope. We are forgiven by Him. We are set free. We no longer have a reason to be downtrodden and without hope, for God has rescued us and lifted us up.

Jehoiachin Was Comforted by the King

Never underestimate the power of a kind word. The Bible tells us that the king of Babylon spoke kindly to Jehoiachin when he released him from prison (see Jer. 52:32). I love this. The king didn't release Jehoiachin and then barrage him with insults, questions or accusations. Perhaps you have had someone say they forgive you but then lay into you with a slew of statements that boil down to, "You don't deserve forgiveness after what you did to me." Or perhaps you have apologized to someone and then they communicate what they really think of you.

On the other hand, God speaks kindly to us. Psalm 3:3 says, "But You, O Lord, are a shield for me, my glory and the One who lifts up my head." He is our comforter and our encourager. When we are hurting, we seek a kind word, don't we? We need a true friend who will understand what we are going through and will lift us up. Jesus is that Friend. He cares when we feel overwhelmed. He cares when we are downcast. And He speaks kindly to us—beckoning for us to rest in His loving care. Solomon wisely shared that "a soft answer turns away wrath, but a harsh word stirs up anger" (Prov. 15:1).

No doubt Jehoiachin had not heard a kind word during his 37 years in prison, but now the king of Babylon was encouraging him through his kindness. In fact, when the king came to the prison cell to let Jehoiachin out, it's quite possible that this former king of Judah feared he would be killed. In contrast, Evil-Merodach, by his kind words, reassured Jehoiachin that he was indeed being set free and that he had found favor with the king of Babylon.

Jehoiachin Was Exalted by the King

The last part of Jeremiah 52:32 says, "And [Evil-Merodach] gave him a more prominent seat than those of the kings who were with him in Babylon." Not only did the king of Babylon speak kindly to Jehoiachin after releasing him from prison, but he also restored his life to what it had been before the enemy took it away. Evil-Merodach exalted Jehoiachin back into a position of authority, making him the most powerful person in Babylon besides himself.

Listen, are you overwhelmed by resentment or bitterness? Do you think your life is over—that it's impossible to rebound from the mess in which you find yourself? I want to remind you that not only does God forgive you, but He also restores you. That is why His forgiveness is so overwhelming and breathtaking. He forgives us, and then He restores our lives. He gives back to us what the enemy has taken. He restores a position of fellowship. He puts us back in a place of leadership—a position of authority. He puts the pieces of our lives back together.

The king of Babylon restored Jehoiachin—and the King of heaven and earth restores us. God's forgiveness brings emotional, mental and even physical healing. He can take us out of that prison, overwhelm us with His forgiveness, and make us new men and women.

Jehoiachin Was Clothed by the King

Jeremiah 52 continues to describe this amazing story: "So Jehoiachin changed from his prison garments" (v. 33). The king of Babylon did not leave Jehoiachin in his prison clothes. He had released him from prison, spoken kindly to him and given him a royal throne—the highest in the kingdom besides his own; thus he could not leave him in prison garb. So the king clothed Jehoiachin in a royal robe—one befitting his new life and position.

That is a picture of what God does for us. He restores our nature, our integrity and our character. He takes away our garment of sadness and gives us a garment of praise. He takes away our garment of darkness and gives us a garment of light. He takes away our filthy rags and gives us a garment of righteousness and purity.

Jehoiachin Was Favored by the King

As the scriptural text describes the next act of mercy on the part of Evil-Merodach, we read that Jehoiachin "ate bread regularly before the king all the days of his life" (Jer. 52:33).

Jehoiachin was favored by the king. When Evil-Merodach set Jehoiachin free and gave him a throne, he didn't say, "Well, it was nice knowing you. Good luck; I hope everything turns out well." Instead, the king communicated, "You are coming with me. You are sticking by my side, and you will eat at the king's table the rest of your life." Evil-Merodach did not abandon Jehoiachin; in fact, by his invitation to eat at his table, Evil-Merodach wanted Jehoiachin to know that they would be friends for the long haul, and that this king of Babylon would be at the one-time king of Judah's side through thick and thin.

When God forgives us—when He takes us out of our pit—He draws us toward Himself. He doesn't let go of us but instead draws us into His presence, into His Word, and into a loving relationship with Him.

You, my reader, are favored by God. He invites you to feast with Him. He invites you to sit with Him. He invites you to be in His presence and hear His voice. To have God's forgiveness overwhelm you means you will find yourself sitting with the King of kings, your life transformed.

Jehoiachin's Future Was Secured by the King

Finally, Jeremiah 52:34 summarizes the final gift that Evil-Merodach lavished upon Jehoiachin: "And as for his provisions, there was a regular ration given him by the king of Babylon, a portion for each day until the day of his death, all the days of his life."

Jehoiachin's future was secured by the king. He had nothing to worry about. Evil-Merodach assured him that he would be taken care of for the rest of his days. What a switch from languishing in prison for 37 years, constantly worrying about whether he would even live another day. Our God has secured our future as well. We have been given the promise of eternal life with Him. Furthermore, we have been given the assurance that we are secure in this life as well—that He will provide for our needs out of the riches of Christ (see Phil. 4:19), and that absolutely nothing will come our way that He doesn't use for our good (see Rom. 8:28).

This is forgiveness. Can you apply forgiveness to your children? Will you apply forgiveness to your spouse? How about to your enemies? It was God's forgiveness that transformed me from a troubled, drug-addicted, angry young guy into a man who many years later would be having dinner with the Supreme Court justices, teaching congressmen and diplomats at the United Nations, and speaking at the White House for the National Day of Prayer.

For you, my friend, the greatest gift in your life is that God has forgiven you. If you will allow yourself to be overwhelmed by this marvelous and astounding truth, you will never be overwhelmed by resentment or bitterness.

STUDY QUESTIONS

1. Christ is our example and model of forgiveness. Describe how Jesus forgives us for our sins. What prevents us from forgiving others as Christ has forgiven us?
2. How does the story about Evil-Merodach and Jehoiachin parallel God's amazing forgiveness toward us?
3. After 37 years of captivity, Jehoiachin was lifted out of prison by the king of Babylon. How does God lift us out of our captivity and set us free?
4. Jehoiachin was exalted by the king and was given a position of authority. In what ways does God exalt us?

∽ PRAYER ∽

Thank You, Lord, that Your work is never incomplete. Thank You that You not only forgive me, but also restore me and replace my filthy rags with Your royal robes of righteousness. You take my broken life and broken dreams and make me new. Help me to be overwhelmed with Your forgiveness today. Help me to be faithful and obedient to then extend that lavish forgiveness toward others. Help me to remember that those who are forgiven much, love much. Fill my heart so completely with Your love that the fragrance of Your Son, Jesus, just oozes from my life. Overwhelm me again, I pray. Amen.

4

Overwhelmed by God's Mercy . . .

instead of ingratitude and indifference

I do not ask the grace which thou didst give to St. Paul;
nor can I dare to ask the grace which thou didst grant to St. Peter;
but, the mercy which thou didst show to the dying robber,
that mercy, show to me.
COPERNICUS

Through the Lord's mercies we are not consumed,
because His compassions fail not.
LAMENTATIONS 3:22

As I've shared before, health issues have plagued me throughout my adult life. Time and time again, I've been in the hospital for various surgeries—six different operations on my knees, replacement of both knees at the same time, surgery on my nose for sleep apnea, and an operation for prostate cancer, among others. Now, because I have been a pastor for more than 40 years and have experienced numerous surgeries, it would seem logical that when I went in for my latest surgery, I would be overwhelmed by God and not by my circumstances, right? Unfortunately, the answer is no. I was in fact overwhelmed by pain and discouragement. But the Lord used my latest stay at the hospital to teach me the importance of being overwhelmed by *Him* rather than by my trials.

The Lord showed me that I easily get overwhelmed with the happenings in my life. If, in my tunnel vision, all I can detect are my problems, then I will be dead in the water, spiritually speaking. In the book of Psalms, David wrote, "Cast your cares on the Lord and he will sustain you; he will never let the righteous be shaken" (Ps. 55:22, *NIV*). In the Hebrew Bible, it explains why: "For it matters to Him concerning you."

The apostle Peter carried this truth into the New Testament when he wrote, "Cast all your anxiety on him because he cares for you" (1 Pet. 5:7, *NIV*). These are great words for us. I would imagine that all of us have times when we don't feel like casting our cares on Him, because we are so overwhelmed. Yet God calls us to bring our anxiety to Him, because even the small stuff matters to Him. When we obey and choose to focus on God's mercy and goodness, our problems find their place in the right perspective.

Being overwhelmed by God means we are not overwhelmed by our problems. I can state emphatically that I have truly been overwhelmed in life, particularly in the area of health. A few years ago, just after my first book with Regal (titled *Overcoming: Discover How to Rise Above and Beyond Your Overwhelming Circumstances in Life!*) came out, it seemed as if everything in my life fell apart. For one thing, the fusion broke in my back. So much for going out and publicizing my new book. I was forced to cancel speaking engagements at churches across the nation. In addition, I had to cancel television and radio interviews that had been scheduled surrounding my book. I even had to cancel a speaking engagement to pastors in London that had been arranged by a professor at a leading university in England.

I had been excited to talk about the message of *Overcoming* to people all over the world, but the Lord had another plan in mind.

It was a desert experience—eight months in the hospital with four different surgeries, and enough pain and trial to kill anyone's flesh. When we talk about God working in our lives, we need to realize that He does what He wants in the affairs of man, for His purposes and His glory. God knows us better than we know ourselves; therefore, He knows when we are ready for growth and sanctification, and also when we are not ready to do a work for Him.

Of all the wonderful character traits that our God possesses, one of my favorites is His mercy. God's grace gives us what we don't deserve. God's mercy, on the other hand, holds back what we actually deserve. Because of His mercy, we are not consumed, we are given a second chance, and we are spared many of the consequences of our actions.

Are you crying out for some mercy today? Would you like to have a little bit of God's kindness in your life—a token, a blessing, a victory over something, or some other outcome that seems to look beyond your sinfulness and misguided attitudes? Do you desire to say to God, "I know that I have been mean, nasty and rotten, but because You do what I don't deserve through Your grace, and You also hold back what I do deserve through Your mercy, perhaps You would show me these today?"

King David Demonstrated God's Mercy

Permit me to share a long but impressive biblical story; it's one of my favorites because it illustrates so powerfully the meaning of mercy and how to apply it:

Now David said, "Is there still anyone who is left of the house of Saul, that I may show him kindness for Jonathan's sake?"

And there was a servant of the house of Saul whose name was Ziba. So when they had called him to David, the king said to him, "Are you Ziba?"

He said, "At your service!"

Then the king said, "Is there not still someone of the house of Saul, to whom I may show the kindness of God?"

And Ziba said to the king, "There is still a son of Jonathan who is lame in his feet."

So the king said to him, "Where is he?"

And Ziba said to the king, "Indeed he is in the house of Machir the son of Ammiel, in Lo Debar."

Then King David sent and brought him out of the house of Machir the son of Ammiel, from Lo Debar.

Now when Mephibosheth the son of Jonathan, the son of Saul, had come to David, he fell on his face and prostrated himself. Then David said, "Mephibosheth?"

And he answered, "Here is your servant!"

So David said to him, "Do not fear, for I will surely show you kindness for Jonathan your father's sake, and will restore to you all the land of Saul your grandfather; and you shall eat bread at my table continually."

Then he bowed himself, and said, "What is your servant, that you should look upon such a dead dog as I?"

And the king called to Ziba, Saul's servant, and said to him, "I have given to your master's son all that belonged to Saul and to all his house. You therefore, and your sons and your servants, shall work the land for him, and you shall bring in the harvest, that your master's son may have food to eat. But Mephibosheth your master's son shall eat bread at my table always." Now Ziba had fifteen sons and twenty servants.

Then Ziba said to the king, "According to all that my lord the king has commanded his servant, so will your servant do."

"As for Mephibosheth," said the king, "he shall eat at my table like one of the king's sons." Mephibosheth had a young son whose name was Micha. And all who dwelt in the house of Ziba were servants of Mephibosheth. So Mephibosheth dwelt in Jerusalem, for he ate continually at the king's table. And he was lame in both his feet (2 Sam. 9:1-13).

The story centers on a young man by the name of Mephibosheth, who was Jonathan's son. After Saul and Jonathan died in battle, the nurse taking care of Mephibosheth (who was five years old at the time) realized that the young boy was in danger of being killed. All of Saul's family had been wiped out, and this wise nurse knew that Mephibosheth would be next. So the nurse took the boy and ran for her life; while running, she tripped and dropped Mephibosheth in such a way that it rendered him lame. No longer did Mephibosheth have the ability to care for himself, so this dear woman took care of him and hid him for the next 16 years.

We humans struggle against being helpless. Yet if we really think about it, we recognize that every one of us needs some type of help. We welcome the prayers of others because of our pain; we yearn for someone to minister to us because we are depressed; or we go through painful and wearisome times—perhaps losing a job, a house or a loved one—and are blessed by the help and encouragement of those around us. Ever since my back issues started plaguing me, for example, I have required help putting on my socks. I no longer have the range of motion I had before, and I cannot even put on my socks by myself. It seems like a little thing, but it is quite discouraging.

After Saul was killed in battle, David became the rightful king over Israel. Upon establishing his throne, David asked if there was anyone left in the house of Saul. Why, so he could wipe them out? No, so he could show mercy! Second Samuel 9:1 opens the story with David's words: "Is there still anyone who is left of the house of Saul, that I may show him kindness for Jonathan's sake?"

Earlier, David and Jonathan had been best friends. In fact, Jonathan was the reason David was able to live as long as he did, because he provided information about what his father's intentions were. Saul, whose actions were highly volatile and unstable, was intent on killing David. He had grown to hate this young man out of envy and wasn't willing to surrender the kingdom. So Saul chased David and had him on the run. It was Jonathan who interceded and helped David escape Saul's murderous intentions. Why didn't David just kill Saul? Because even though David knew that God had anointed him for the throne, he also recognized that for the time being, Saul was God's anointed. David wasn't willing to disobey God. In spite of Saul's hatred and attempts to murder him, David still respected the Lord's anointing over King Saul.

In fact, David had to wait years, living as a fugitive inside of caves until the day that Jonathan and Saul died, before he could take his rightful, God-anointed place on the throne of the kingdom of Israel.

All of that being the case, normal human logic dictates that David, when finally on the throne, would seek revenge and ensure that Saul's family was completely wiped out. Amazingly, the opposite was true. Because of his love for Jonathan, David wanted to bless and show kindness to whoever was remaining in Saul's family. Ultimately, David desired to show mercy to Saul's family instead of revenge.

Second Samuel 9:6-7 relates what transpired when Jonathan's son was brought before David's throne: "When Mephibosheth ... had come to David, he fell on his face and prostrated himself. Then David said, 'Mephibosheth?'

"And he answered, 'Here is your servant!'

"So David said to him, 'Do not fear, for I will surely show you kindness.'"

David requested, "Is there anyone whom I can bless? Is there anyone whom I can shower with kindness?" Notice that it didn't make any difference to David what Saul or any member of Saul's family had done. David didn't care if the person left in Saul's family was criticizing him or murmuring or griping against the throne. David wanted to show mercy—the kindness of God.

Is this the type of mercy you desperately desire to experience in your life today? Could you use a dose of God's kindness? Turn to Him. He's waiting to show you His never-failing mercy and kindness.

Now, it's important to make something very clear: God's mercy is extended to us for one reason—because of His Son, Jesus Christ. If we believe in Christ—if we turn to Him—then we will experience God's mercy. David extended mercy to Mephibosheth not because Mephibosheth was lame, but because he was the son of Jonathan. David told this man that he could continually sit at the king's table. He not only showed mercy, but he also honored Mephibosheth by eating meals with him on a daily basis. I would imagine that David, in his kindness, covered Mephibosheth's legs with a royal tapestry, so that all the people in David's court could see him only from the waist up, thus sparing the young man any kind of shame or embarrassment.

Likewise, when God shows us His mercy, He covers the shame of our sin with His blood; He restores everything that people have taken; and He sits us at His royal table, calling us "friend."

Consider how it must have felt for this crippled fellow, who had been in hiding for 16 years, to suddenly find himself sitting at the king's table. Mephibosheth went from being a fugitive to becoming an integral part of David's kingdom. The same thing happens when God gets a hold of us. He sits us at His table, and we become famous—not famous with people, necessarily, but famous with God. And when we become famous with God, God begins to do great exploits through our lives.

David demonstrated God's mercy. He could have destroyed Mephibosheth as his enemy, but he chose instead to shower him with kindness, mercy and blessings. So how does this powerful principle translate into our lives today? Perhaps you are upset at your new son-in-law for taking your daughter away, or maybe you're enraged at your ex-husband because he divorced you and took the kids away. You have a choice to make. You can live in bitterness, or you can extend God's mercy toward that person and experience God's wonderful work in you. Remember the mercy that God has already shown you. Although you are crippled, you are blessed. Although you are not doing what you should be, God is showing you favor.

We are told in 1 Corinthians 13:7 that love "bears all things, believes all things, hopes all things, endures all things." If we are going to extend mercy to others, we must believe God at His Word and that He is in control of all things. Our hope is in Him, and when we understand these fundamentals, we are able to love in such a way that endures through hard times.

God's Mercy and Grace
Work Together to Restore

God is ready to bestow His wonderful mercy and kindness on us. His grace and mercy go hand in hand, and together these gifts of God do a work of restoration and beauty. Most believers sense the necessity for God's grace and mercy. Let's examine five specific conditions in which we feel our neediness most keenly—drawing from the example and story of Mephibosheth.

When We Are Miserable

Before David extended mercy to him, Mephibosheth was miserable and cursed. He had been in hiding for 16 years because he was a wanted man. He knew that David was now on the throne and that he was the only family member left of the house of Saul. Mephibosheth had been rendered lame because of his fall. But he was the son of Jonathan, and because of that, he had an inheritance. Mephibosheth experienced God's mercy and grace through King David. Instead of a death sentence, he was given life.

In the same way, we are miserable prior to knowing God. We are overwhelmed by our condition and filled with ingratitude and sin. But when we come to God, we experience God's mercy and grace through His Son, Jesus Christ. Instead of death, we are given life—an eternal inheritance. God's mercy extends to us when we are miserable.

When We Are Fearful

Mephibosheth certainly wasn't expecting mercy from King David. For 16 years, he had been in hiding, afraid that his life would be taken, just like the rest of the house of Saul. When he first heard that King David was inquiring about any survivors from Saul's family, he likely trembled in fear. After all, Mephibosheth would expect to be killed, as the rest of his family had been earlier. But David made it clear that he was looking for a relative of Saul so that he could show mercy and kindness.

Are you fearful? Are you overwhelmed? God is seeking you out to show you His mercy. Maybe, like Mephibosheth, you are running away—fleeing and hiding from God because you are afraid that He is just waiting to clobber you. But that is the opposite of the heart of God toward you. He wants to extend mercy to you and show you His kindness. God is asking, "Do you want to get saved? Do you want to get right with Me? Come to Me so that I can make your heart clean and your path straight."

God is on a quest to touch our hearts; He asks us to give Him all our burdens and sorrows so that He can replace them with His joy. He'll take the heaviness away and make our feet light to dance (see Ps. 30:11). God doesn't want us to be overwhelmed by life's issues, struggles and fears. He wants us to be overwhelmed with *Him* so that we can have an abundant life.

When We Are Destitute

Second Samuel 9:8 describes Mephibosheth's posture and attitude of self-condemnation as he approached David's throne: "Then he bowed himself, and said, 'What is your servant, that you should look upon such a dead dog as I?'"

Mephibosheth was a humble man. He was destitute and knew that he brought nothing to the king's throne. He couldn't understand why someone of King David's stature would want to extend so much kindness to a man of his disposition.

If only we had such an attitude of humility when approaching God! Sometimes we act as if we are the top dog—instead of the destitute people we really are when we do not have Christ in our life. When we realize that we cannot help ourselves—that we are destitute—we can humbly come to God and petition His mercy to lift us up. The apostle Paul tells us that through our weaknesses, He makes us strong (see 2 Cor. 12:9).

Making a decision or moving forward without God's direction is not wise. It's a fitting thing to be dependent on a sovereign God who loves us. For example, when God called Moses to lead the Israelite people out of Egypt, Moses had the same attitude as Mephibosheth, asking, "Who am I?" (Exod. 3:11). Moses definitely resisted God's call to leadership, even going so far as to say, "Please send someone else" (Exod. 4:13, *NIV*). Similarly, Mephibosheth recognized his own state of being bereft and bankrupt, humbling himself before the king and then experiencing rich mercy, kindness, and a changed life.

When We Are Separated

Mephibosheth had been separated from his people, his place of worship and his homeland of Jerusalem for years, because he was in hiding. In much the same way, prior to knowing Christ, we are separated from God. Even as believers, we can slip out of fellowship with God or revert to ungodly ways of behaving. When we move away from Christ, we can't hear His voice. So the Holy Spirit goes after us to bring us back into fellowship. Second Samuel 9:5 shows this same type of pursuit: "King David sent and brought [Mephibosheth] out of the house of Machir the son of Ammiel, from Lo Debar."

King David sought after Mephibosheth. So, too, does the God of all creation seek after each of us, desiring to overwhelm us with His great mercy and kindness. When we understand that, how can we be overwhelmed by problems and troubles?

When We Are Helpless

Mephibosheth was lame and crippled; he required help not only with his daily care, but also just to be able to move about. King David had to send for him, and when Mephibosheth was brought to his royal table, David ensured that the young man was helped in every way. God never ignores our helplessness. When Jesus walked the earth, He constantly reached out to those who were helpless—helpless in their sin and spiritual impoverishment, helpless in their physical incapacity and/or helpless in their mental distress. The crowds often ignored the helpless and the destitute, but not Jesus. He loved them and helped them as a result of His love.

We are all helpless in one way or another. We often get overwhelmed because we realize that we are helpless to change our circumstances. But instead of allowing depression and anxiety to overcome us, we should realize that our helplessness is God's opportunity to do a great work in our lives. That's one marvelous facet of our God's nature. He reaches down, picks us up and places us on stable ground.

Are you feeling weak or helpless? God is ready to bestow His wonderful mercy and kindness on you. Read these compelling words of the apostle Paul: "Now to Him who is able to do exceedingly abundantly above all that we ask or think, according to the power that works in us, to Him be glory in the church by Christ Jesus to all generations, forever and ever. Amen" (Eph. 3:20-21).

Mercy = Love

What animates God's mercy toward us? Without a doubt, the driving force behind God's mercy is His abundant love for us. His love is spontaneous and unconditional.

When the robber on the cross next to Jesus said, "Lord, remember me when You come into Your kingdom," Jesus didn't give him a laundry list of things he had to do in order for God's mercy to extend toward him! Rather, Jesus turned to the man and said, "Today you will be with Me in Paradise" (Luke 23:42-43).

The Bible shares the exceedingly good news that "while we were still sinners, Christ died for us" (Rom. 5:8). God's love is instant. It's not based on what we look like, what we do, or what we have. And His love and kindness draw us to Him (see Rom. 2:4).

King David planned on extending mercy and kindness to Mephibosheth before he even knew him. It didn't matter that Mephibosheth was lame or destitute. David's love for Jonathan's son was spontaneous, just as God's love is for us.

God's love and mercy are also gracious and sacrificial. The fact that God gave us the gift of salvation without our doing one single thing proves His abundant love for us. The fact that Jesus willingly gave up His life on the cross so that we could be forgiven of our sins, which we could never atone for on our own, shows the extent of God's love.

King David loved Mephibosheth. His love was spontaneous, gracious, generous and sacrificial. David brought Jonathan's son into his kingdom and put him at a place of honor at his table on a daily basis. He ensured that Mephibosheth was taken care of and had all the help he needed. He gave up his rights to Saul's possessions and riches, giving them instead to Mephibosheth, ensuring that the young man had an inheritance.

That is mercy. That's what mercy does. Are you feeling overwhelmed? Be overwhelmed by God's mercy instead. God is reaching out to you with His mercy and kindness, wanting to bless you and lead you down the right path. Take His ever-present hand and let His great love lead you on through the troubles in your life.

STUDY QUESTIONS

1. Explain how David demonstrated God's mercy toward Mephibosheth.
2. In what ways does God's mercy extend to us when we are miserable?
3. What is God's heart toward those who are overwhelmed with fear?
4. What drives God's mercy toward us?

∾ PRAYER ∾

Thank You, Lord, that Your love is sacrificial, generous and unsolicited. You loved me first. Your mercy is new to me every day, and it refreshes me when I feel I cannot go on. Thank You that You do not leave me alone to accept many of the consequences of my own actions, but You spare me for Your name's sake. You are always working things out for my good—not for my comfort or pleasure, but for my good, so that I may be more like Jesus. Thank You that You love me in spite of myself. May Your mercy toward me cause me to love others and be a witness to everyone I meet. Be glorified in my life today, I pray. Amen.

5

Overwhelmed by God's Purpose . . .

instead of the things of this world

*To experience the glory of God's will for us means absolute trust.
It means the will to do His will, and it means joy.*
ELISABETH ELLIOT

*For I have come down from heaven, not to do My own will,
but the will of Him who sent Me.*
JOHN 6:38

What is the purpose of God for your life? Have you ever asked that question? Have you ever wondered why you are here on this earth and why you are who you are? God created you for a reason. It's amazing, really: He has both a purpose and a plan for you; hence, you are uniquely formed and fashioned as an individual. Your purpose and life plans are just as unique.

Through His matchless and handcrafted design, God made you to be ideally suited for His purposes for you. Not only did He create you with precision and care, but He also continues His work in your life on a day-to-day basis. He knows your heart and your innermost thoughts and desires; this is exactly what the writer to the Hebrew

79

Christians communicates in Hebrews 4:12: "For the word of God is living and powerful, and sharper than any two-edged sword, piercing even to the division of soul and spirit, and of joints and marrow, and is a discerner of the thoughts and intents of the heart."

Now, go back and read that Scripture verse again. Look intently at every single word because it is the great revelation of God concerning what He can do in our lives. It seems reasonable to think that we, knowing Him as Creator, would surrender to whatever God wants to do in our lives, but too often we don't. Pridefully, we think we know what is best; therefore, we frequently fight against God's will and purpose instead of submitting to them.

The Bible says that we are God's workmanship. The apostle Paul explained this concept in his letter to the people in Ephesus: "For we are His workmanship, created in Christ Jesus for good works, which God prepared beforehand that we should walk in them" (Eph. 2:10). This word "workmanship" is the translation of the Greek term *poima*, which means that each of us is God's work of art. We are God's poem—His beautiful creation. God had something special in mind when He made each person.

Sometimes we are not happy with how God made us. We think, *God, why did You make me look this way?* or *Why didn't You give me more brains?* or *Why can't I be more like so-and-so?* We can even get angry with God about how He created us. But God made each of us the way we are for a purpose. He loves us and knows us better than we know ourselves. We will never be happy and fulfilled until we are in the center of God's will for our lives.

God's Purpose: Fulfilling His Will

As we dive into the concept of fulfilling God's purpose and will, let's examine a passage from the Gospel of Matthew. In this dramatic scene, we read:

And suddenly, one of those who were with Jesus stretched out his hand and drew his sword, struck the servant of the high priest, and cut off his ear.

But Jesus said to him, "Put your sword in its place, for all who take the sword will perish by the sword. Or do you think that I cannot now pray to My Father, and He will provide Me with more than twelve legions of angels? How then could the Scriptures be fulfilled, that it must happen thus?" (Matt. 26:51-54).

The Gospel of John records that the man who cut off the ear of the high priest's servant was Peter (see John 18:10). I find it amusing that Peter, who was a fisherman by trade, had a sword. These verses describe the night before Jesus' crucifixion, when He was in the Garden of Gethsemane and was being betrayed by Judas, who led a crowd to arrest Jesus. Peter obviously was not good at using a sword, because he swiped off the ear of the servant of the high priest instead of taking him out.

When we are doing what God has equipped us to do—living with and operating in the gifting He has given to us—great things happen in our lives. But when we try to be someone other than the person God has created us to be or covet another's position rather than embracing the role He has given us, things begin to crumble. Marriages suffer, children suffer, our walk with the Lord suffers, and other people start "losing ears"—all because we are not where God wants us. So before we give Peter a hard time, we need to ask ourselves, *How many ears have I lopped off in my Christian life while fighting against God?*

Jesus' comments to Peter are very revealing when it comes to God's will for our lives. He told Peter that those who use the sword will die by the sword. In other words, if we fight against God's will, we are going to perish. Furthermore, Jesus reminded Peter that if

God wanted to rescue Him from the situation He was in, God was able to do so without man's help. Should Jesus rely on Peter's sword or on 12 legions of angels to rescue Him? A legion, by the way, numbers 6,000, so 12 legions would be 72,000 angels.

The greater question, however, was whether Jesus wanted to be rescued from the situation. The disciples certainly didn't want Jesus to be taken and imprisoned; they definitely did not want Jesus to die. Even Jesus Himself had asked just hours earlier, while praying alone in the Garden of Gethsemane, if His Father would take away the burden of the cross. But ultimately, Jesus' greatest desire was to fulfill the will of God in His life, not to escape the unfathomably difficult and painful trial He knew was ahead.

Do you want to be rescued? Do you really want to escape the trials that you are facing right now? Someone is likely thinking, *Yes! I don't like living with my husband; I don't like suffering what I'm going through; I don't like how the kids are behaving right now.*

If that's what you're thinking, I would ask you, "Okay, so what are you going to do?"

If your response is, "I'm going to leave," I would challenge you with the fact that you are married; you have kids; you have a responsibility. The reality is that in spite of your feeling an urge to escape, that is not God's will for you.

Jesus asked a probing question: "How then could the Scriptures be fulfilled, that it must happen thus?" (Matt. 26:54). Jesus let it be known that God was completely able to rescue Him out of the situation if that were His will. But the truth was that God's will for Jesus culminated in His arrest and death on the cross. Jesus knew that the purpose and plan for His life included a final, very painful trial. It indeed was God's will for Jesus to go to the cross; Jesus understood that fact and was committed to God's will for His life.

God's will is definitely not running away, swinging a sword or trying to escape. Then what is God's will? He wants us to face what we're facing and to fulfill what He created us to fulfill.

During the time when I was in bed in the hospital and wanted nothing more than to escape my pain, God said, "Steve, *face it and fulfill it.*" The spiritual point is that it didn't matter if my strength was forever diminished, or if my body was not what it was before. What mattered was this: Will I accept it? If we allow God to fulfill His will in our lives, we will find true peace and true joy.

I found myself arguing, "But I don't want that, Lord. I want a healthy body." Swinging the sword and fighting God's will made me miserable.

Jesus told Peter that He would fulfill what was His to fulfill because He was firmly set on accomplishing the Father's will; He knew what His purpose in life was and that God's plan was the only way to go. Knowing God and understanding His greater purpose for our lives helps us accept the difficult situations that come our way without being overwhelmed. When we are overwhelmed by knowing and living God's purpose for our lives, running or fighting against God's will becomes unnecessary. Being firmly committed to God's purpose, in fact, helps us stop running and start facing the difficult issues. So for the married person, he should fulfill that relationship by dying to himself and selflessly loving his spouse. For the mother, she should stop running and fulfill her responsibility as a nurturing parent. No doubt hardships are formidable and wearisome to face. Swinging the sword or running away seems much easier. *But that is not God's will.*

The biblical story of Jonah is famous because of the great lengths this prophet employed to avoid God's will for his life. Instead of going to Nineveh as God had commanded him to do, Jonah "ran away from the Lord and headed for Tarshish" (Jon. 1:3, *NIV*), jumping on a boat in hopes of getting far away from what God wanted him to do. It's funny, isn't it, that we think we can run away from God and He won't find us.

When the boat Jonah was on encountered a bad storm, Jonah knew he was the cause of that storm. Upon Jonah's suggestion, the ship's crew threw him overboard. Yet Jonah could not escape God's presence even under the sea, as God orchestrated that a large fish swallow Jonah—whole! After spending three days and nights in the belly of the fish, Jonah finally surrendered to God and agreed to obey Him. As soon as the fish spat Jonah out on the land, God reiterated His original instruction: "Go to Nineveh."

Are you wasting time, running away from what God wants you to do? Or are you still trying to figure out what it is that God wants to do through your life?

We read in Romans 8:28, "And we know that all things work together for good to those who love God, to those who are the called according to His purpose." Are you called? If you are a child of God, then yes, you are! Do you love God? I hope the answer to this question is also yes. Then God will work everything—which includes all the trials, hardships and difficult situations—out for good in your life. In Ecclesiastes 3:11, we read, "He has made everything beautiful in its time. Also He has put eternity in [men's] hearts, except that no one can find out the work that God does from beginning to end." In other words, God puts a work of His choosing in our hearts and is faithful to show us His will if we are seeking it.

God's Purpose: A Loving Relationship with Him

We have established that God has called us and has a purpose and will for each of us. He wants us to understand His will so that He can fulfill His plan in our lives. Ephesians 1:4 spells out an amazing truth: "He chose us in Him before the foundation of the world, that we should be holy and without blame before Him in love."

84

It's important to repeat what the apostle Paul says. God chose us before the foundations of the earth were created. We were chosen to be made right with God—blameless through Jesus Christ—and to have a loving relationship with Him.

Ephesians 1:5-6 continues: "Having predestined us to adoption as sons by Jesus Christ to Himself, according to the good pleasure of His will, to the praise of the glory of His grace, by which He made us accepted in the Beloved." So, not only were we chosen to be made right with God and to have a loving relationship with Him, but we were also adopted into God's family and accepted as we are by the Lord. Meditating on this amazing truth should cause us to question how we can ever feel rejected. How can we ever feel like an "accident"? Each of us was uniquely created by God with a divine purpose to know Him, to be loved by Him, to be adopted into His family and to be accepted by Him.

Ephesians 1:9-12 finalizes these amazing truths:

Having made known to us the mystery of His will, according to His good pleasure which He purposed in Himself, that in the dispensation of the fullness of the times He might gather together in one all things in Christ, both which are in heaven and which are on earth—in Him. In Him also we have obtained an inheritance, being predestined according to the purpose of Him who works all things according to the counsel of His will, that we who first trusted in Christ should be to the praise of His glory.

God wants us to understand that He adopted us, accepted us, chose us, and wants a close, loving relationship with us—one in which He is glorified through the accomplishment of His will in our lives. Let's take a closer look at four reasons why God, in His purpose, created each one of us.

Created to Love Him

We were made to have a relationship with the living God. In fact, God loves each of us so much that He sacrificed His only Son to ensure that we would no longer be separated from Him. In return, He wants our love. Mark 12:30 says, "'And you shall love the Lord your God with all your heart, with all your soul, with all your mind, and with all your strength.' This is the first commandment." The God who created us wants us to love Him with all our heart, soul, mind and strength. In other words, the Lord comes first in our lives. It is vital that we seek to love and know Him, because we were created for this purpose.

Created to Serve and Praise Him

Deuteronomy 10:12 says, "And now, Israel, what does the Lord your God require of you, but to fear the Lord your God, to walk in all His ways and to love Him, to serve the Lord your God with all your heart and with all your soul."

God chose each of us before we were even born. In fact, before the foundations of the earth were formed, He had in mind every person who has ever existed. He predestined that each of us would be part of His overall plan. This verse in Deuteronomy gives a crystal-clear picture of what God wants for us in our daily lives. He wants us to fear Him, which means acknowledging Him with humility and awe and respecting His authority in our lives. He also desires that we walk in His ways—being obedient to His Word and bearing the fruit of the Holy Spirit in how we live—and that we love Him.

Finally, the verse specifies that God wants us to serve Him with all our heart and soul. No matter where the Lord places us, we are to serve Him wholeheartedly. Whether as a CEO, a business executive, an administrative assistant, a computer techie, a hairstylist, a teacher, a stay-at-home mom or in any other role or position, God wants us to fulfill our given roles as if we were working directly for Him. When we serve God this way, with all our heart and soul, everything we do should be done with joy and to bring Him glory. By the way, God created the order of the universe this way—that each of us would bring praise and glory to Him.

So God made us to do one thing exceptionally well: to praise Him. He didn't create us to figure everything out. We run into trouble and get easily overwhelmed because we don't know what the future holds, and we strive to figure it out. A better idea is to trust that we are made in the image of God and that God has a master plan for us—not to worry about what's ahead. God has it all figured out. So why are we worried? In fact, we get especially overwhelmed when events unfold in a way that runs counter to how we think they should, or when our situation doesn't make any sense in our human mind. To God, however, everything makes perfect sense and fits perfectly in place.

Created to Walk with Him

The prophet Micah further enlightens us on what the Lord desires from His followers: "He has shown you, O man, what is good; and what does the Lord require of you but to do justly, to love mercy, and to walk humbly with your God?" (Mic. 6:8).

Here, Micah outlines the way in which we are to walk with the Lord. First, we are to do justly, which means we are to do what is right in the eyes of the Lord. How do we know what is right? By reading and meditating on His Word, and by following His example. Jesus didn't sin, and though we will never be sinless, we can rely on the power of the Holy Spirit to help us live a pure and obedient life. In addition, we are to love mercy, which means we are to be compassionate, caring and kind to those around us, just as the Lord is to us. Finally, we are to walk humbly with our God, which means never forgetting that we are sinners saved by grace. Because of God's glorious sacrifice, we have been given the gift of eternal life. The Lord wants us to be people of humility—a trait that demon-strates the heart of God (see Phil. 2:5-8).

Created to Be His Workmanship

In Ephesians 2, we read, "But God, who is rich in mercy, because of His great love with which He loved us, even when we were dead in trespasses, made us alive together with Christ (by grace you have been saved). . . . For we are His workmanship, created in Christ Jesus for good works, which God prepared beforehand that we should walk in them" (vv. 4-5,10).

This verse clearly communicates that we were created by God to do good works through Jesus Christ. We are His workmanship. We are created—fashioned, molded—in His image. This biblical truth is reit-erated in John 1:3: "All things were made through Him, and without Him nothing was made that was made," and in Colossians 1:16: "For by Him all things were created that are in heaven and that are on earth, visible and invisible, whether thrones or dominions or princi-palities or powers. All things were created through Him and for Him."

We humans so often think that it is our job to help God out in His creation, don't we? "Lord, I have a few suggestions as to how You should have formed me." In spite of our misguided thinking, God doesn't need our input on what He should do in our lives. If we would stop fighting Him and submit to His plan, we would find true peace and happiness—resting in the truth that "if anyone is in Christ, he is a new creation; old things have passed away; behold, all things have become new" (2 Cor. 5:17).

God made us—He is the Creator. So why do we worry about or question what the Lord is doing? Rather, we should pay close atten-tion to and apply the principle found in these verses in Jeremiah 18:

> Then I went down to the potter's house, and there he was,
> making something at the wheel. And the vessel that he made

88

of clay was marred in the hand of the potter; so he made it again into another vessel, as it seemed good to the potter to make.

Then the word of the Lord came to me, saying: "O house of Israel, can I not do with you as this potter?" says the Lord. "Look, as the clay is in the potter's hand, so are you in My hand, O house of Israel!" (vv. 3-6).

What is this principle? God is the Potter, and we are the clay. So who controls what happens in our lives? God sovereignly controls. Who controls the speed of the wheel? God expertly controls. Who is shaping each of us with His hands? God is shaping and fashioning us as seems good to Him. The Lord knows exactly what He is doing—He uses every circumstance, every trial and every hardship to mold us into the men and women that He has planned for us to be.

We need to stop questioning what God is making. The following "conversation" with God might seem silly, but it has a point:

"God, what are You making?"

"I'm going to make a coffee cup."

"But I don't want to be a coffee cup; I want to be an ash tray."

"No, Stephen, you're not going to be an ash tray."

"But I *want* to be an ash tray."

"No, you're going to be a coffee cup."

"God, I think You're wrong."

I keep arguing with Him, but He just dips His hand in the water, gets the pottery wheel going faster and faster, and flattens me out like a pancake. As He works, God says, "You're not going to be an ash tray, and by the way, why are you questioning Me? Why is the clay telling the Potter what to do? I had a plan for you before you were even born, and you've been fighting Me every step of the way for 60 years. When are you going to stop fighting Me and start trusting Me?"

I encourage you to yield to God instead of fighting Him. Let Him fashion you into what He has purposed and planned for you to be, so that you are a vessel who not only brings Him glory, but also blesses all the people around you. God wants you to quit swinging the sword and to stop running away from His will. Instead, face the tough issues in each season and submit to God's pruning and shaping, so that you can fulfill the call and will of God. The Potter knows what He wants to do. You are His *poima*—His work of art. You are a very special person. Let God make you into the person He wants you to be and fulfill His purpose through you.

STUDY QUESTIONS

1. What will we find when we allow God to fulfill His will in our lives?
2. When we know God and understand His greater purpose for our lives, what happens?
3. Name the four reasons why God created you.
4. What is God's purpose for us, and what kind of relationship does God want with us?

∽ PRAYER ∽

Lord, I am Your workmanship, Your tapestry, Your work of art. Thank You that everything You make is good and will come to an expected end. Thank You that You do not leave me as a heavy, ugly lump of clay, but are forming me into an incredible instrument for Your glory. Don't let me go, Lord. Even if at times I complain, murmur and argue, please forgive me and do not take Your hands off of my life. Lord, I submit to Your will today. Have Your way with me, Lord, for Your plans and purposes are the only way I will be truly fulfilled and find peace. Overwhelm me with Your touch and with Your purpose for my life, I pray. Amen.

6

Overwhelmed by God's Power . . .

instead of temptation and sin

You do not test the resources of God until you try the impossible.

F. B. MEYER

But you shall receive power when the Holy Spirit has come upon you;
and you shall be witnesses to Me in Jerusalem, and in all Judea
and Samaria, and to the end of the earth.

ACTS 1:8

Wouldn't it be nice if we stopped being overwhelmed by all of our problems and instead had such a close relationship with God that we allowed His power to infuse us to make changes in our homes, families, communities, workplaces, churches and nations?

God has so changed my heart that I don't want to spend time being overwhelmed by the difficult circumstances in my life; they will always be there in one way or another. Usually we get through one trial only to find there is another one waiting. One problem resolves, and there is always another on the horizon. In fact, I've heard it said that at any given time, a person is either entering into a trial, in a trial, or coming out of a trial. Perhaps this sounds pessimistic or negative, but it is indeed a reality. We will never have a

93

problem-free, trial-free life. That's exactly why it's critical to stop living in a state in which we are overwhelmed by the problems in our lives. Remaining stuck in that frame of mind reflects an immature faith that doesn't take into account the glorious and powerful God we serve.

Jesus certainly didn't live a trouble-free existence. But He relied on the goodness and power of God throughout His lifetime on earth. Jesus chose to be overwhelmed by God and not by the trials and evil that He faced on a daily basis.

These trials were multiple and never-ending. Consider this list: He was tempted by Satan for 40 days and nights; He was constantly questioned, ridiculed and mocked by the religious leaders of the day; He was confronted with wickedness and demons in many of the places that He went to minister; He was betrayed by someone close to Him; He sweated great drops of blood in the Garden of Gethsemane; He was arrested and beaten ruthlessly; He was subjected to an illegal trial; He was spat on; He was rejected by His own people; He was separated from His heavenly Father for our sake; He bore the iniquities and sin of all people, even though He was innocent; and He was crucified on a cross—suffering an agonizing death. Yet through it all, Jesus loved, ministered and never faltered. Why? Because He was overwhelmed by His heavenly Father.

So here are my questions for you:

- Are you overwhelmed by your problems and challenging situations?
- Are you overwhelmed by your business or job or lack of finances?
- Are you overwhelmed by your family or relationships?
- *Or are you overwhelmed by how great God is and by His power and person?*

God's Power to Lift Us Up and Keep Us Going

Marvel with me over these truths and promises from the book of Isaiah:

> Have you not known? Have you not heard? The everlasting God, the Lord, the Creator of the ends of the earth, neither faints nor is weary. His understanding is unsearchable. He gives power to the weak, and to those who have no might He increases strength. Even the youths shall faint and be weary, and the young men shall utterly fall, but those who wait on the Lord shall renew their strength; they shall mount up with wings like eagles, they shall run and not be weary, they shall walk and not faint (Isa. 40:28-31).

The God who made the heavens and the earth *does not faint*. Nothing overtakes Him or saps His strength. On the other hand, we humans experience many moments when we grow faint. We get to a point at which we feel like we just can't handle another day. We find ourselves exhausted and worn out, tired of thinking, and weary of re-lating—and sadly, it doesn't take much for us to feel this way. In fact, we can get so overwhelmed that when someone takes a parking space we had our eye on, we explode. That's how uptight and stressed out we are. But is that what God wants in our lives? No, He wants us to use the power He gives us—His power—to take our eyes off of the "stuff" that is going on around us and to focus instead on Him. It is God who gives power to the weak and strength to those who are exhausted.

Are you feeling weak? God will give you power to rise above the obstacles in your path. Feeling exhausted? God will give you the strength you need to keep going.

There is no reason for us to be "weak" Christians, walking around with our heads hanging low, crying, "Woe is me!" The key to overcom-ing weakness, sin, temptation and weariness is to wait on the Lord.

That means focusing on intimacy with God by reading His Word daily, communicating with Him through prayer, fellowshipping with other believers, and setting our minds on His greatness rather than our problems. The Scripture in Isaiah is crystal-clear: When we wait on the Lord, our strength is renewed, we rise above our problems, we run and don't grow weary, and we walk without becoming faint.

Jeremiah 12:5 poses the question: "If you have run with the footmen, and they have wearied you, then how can you contend with horses?" In other words, if we are overwhelmed by the relatively small, everyday problems in life, how are we going to be able to handle the bigger, foundation-shaking issues that will likely come our way? God is asking Jeremiah, "What are you going to do, Jeremiah? You're beginning to complain about what's happening in your life. Do you see the problem, or do you see Me? Are you focusing on the situation and how tired you are, or are you looking at the strength I'll give you to overcome it? And by the way, Jeremiah, I'll never give you anything that I won't also give you the power to overcome. You have the ability, through Me, to do great things and go far beyond what you think is possible." That's the attitude God desires to ring loudly in our hearts.

God's Power over the Enemy

Some of the battles we confront are of our own making. But we also face a real enemy, Satan, whose goals are to deter us in our faith and destroy our walk with the Lord. If Satan came after Jesus, he will surely come after us. But Jesus dealt with Satan in a powerful way; Matthew 4:10 recounts what Jesus said to His enemy: "Away with you, Satan! For it is written, 'You shall worship the Lord your God, and Him only you shall serve.'" Jesus spent 40 days in the desert without food, and when He was tired and hungry, Satan began his attack. Isn't that true to form? Usually we face the greatest attacks from the enemy when we are tired, stressed and battling significant problems. Satan almost always ambushes us when we are at our most vulnerable.

Even though Jesus was physically weak from hunger, He had the spiritual power to resist Satan's temptations. He didn't shout; He didn't call down thunder and lightning; He didn't display a huge emotional outburst. Instead He forcefully countered Satan's lies with the truth of God's Word. In the same way, through the power of the Holy Spirit residing in us, no matter how physically, emotionally or mentally weak we may feel, we can resist the attacks of the enemy through the truth of God's Word.

First Peter 5:8 urges us: "Be sober, be vigilant; because your adversary the devil walks about like a roaring lion, seeking whom he may devour." We must be aware of spiritual warfare; it's critical to understand when we are being attacked by spiritual forces of darkness. The devil's intentions are to destroy our walk with the Lord. He plans to wreak havoc in our lives. This doesn't mean that we should be afraid, or that Satan is behind everything bad that happens to us. Still, being aware of the enemy's tactics and knowing the truth of God's Word are vital.

An important question to ask in every circumstance is this: "What is the will of God for me in this situation?" We know that it is wrong to steal, lie, commit adultery or fornication, hurt someone, slander, gossip, lust, and so on. So when we find ourselves being tempted in an area that can lead to sin, we must stand firm on the truth of God's Word and do what is right. The apostle James instructs, "Therefore submit to God. Resist the devil and he will flee from you" (Jas. 4:7). Notice that the verse says "resist" and not "dabble with" or "flirt with." Too often we play with temptation instead of resisting it. Is it any wonder the devil does not flee from us?

I sometimes hear this question: "But, Pastor Steve, how do we 'resist' when the temptation is so strong?" The answer is that we submit ourselves to God, wholly and completely. We choose to do God's will instead of our own. We seek to please God instead of our flesh. God is committed to giving us the power to resist the devil and temptation when we are submitting and surrendering ourselves to Him. But trying to wage this battle against the enemy through our own strength will indeed lead to failure.

In Ephesians 6:11-12, the apostle Paul exhorts believers to "put on the whole armor of God, that you may be able to stand against the wiles of the devil. For we do not wrestle against flesh and blood, but against principalities, against powers, against the rulers of the darkness of this age, against spiritual hosts of wickedness in the heavenly places." In multiple places, the Scriptures make it clear that we have an enemy who is seeking to ruin our lives and especially to destroy our fellowship with God. He uses lies to try to turn us away from our heavenly Father: "You know God doesn't love you. If He loved you, He would have never allowed these struggles to happen."

It is critical to counter the lies of the enemy with God's truth: "No, God does love me, and He wants to work in and through my life. He will use these trials to bring about His good will."

We must stop listening to the lies of the enemy and rely on the truth of God's Word instead. God does not want us to be overwhelmed with problems. God does not want us to be stressed out or be an emotional basket case. Rather, the Lord wants us to immerse ourselves in Him, so that we have His peace and joy regardless of the troubles and circumstances we find ourselves facing.

I read an interesting story recently about the release procedure for patients in a mental hospital. In a decent-sized room, the doctor would turn on a faucet and hand the patient a mop. If the patient immediately began to mop, attempting to clean up the mess without first turning off the spigot, he or she would not be released. This was evidence that the patient was not thinking through the situation clearly, or that he or she could not put two and two together.

The reality is that many of us, even Christians, do this in our spiritual lives. We are given a mop of truth, and we try to use it to clean up our mess—but we have not turned off the faucet of evil pouring into our hearts and lives. Like this mental-hospital patient, we disqualify ourselves from obtaining our freedom. God's power is available to us to conquer our weaknesses, to resist temptations, and to defeat the enemy, but we *must* say no to sin and yes to God.

The Power of God at Work in Our Lives

Practically speaking, how does the power of God work in our lives? Let's examine eight examples from Scripture that show just how God's power helps us on a day-to-day basis.

God Will Keep Us in All Places

Genesis 28:15-16 shares a beautiful promise from the Lord: "'Behold, I am with you and will keep you wherever you go, and will bring you back to this land; for I will not leave you until I have done what I have spoken to you.'

"Then Jacob awoke from his sleep and said, 'Surely the Lord is in this place, and I did not know it.'"

Just as He was with Jacob, God is with us wherever we go. He's with us at church, at home, at work, in the hospital and in the car. No matter where we go, the Lord is right there with us—He never lets us out of His sight. That can either make us feel completely secure, or it can make us nervous, depending on the types of things we do and the places we visit. Too often, we don't realize that God is right here with us in *this* place.

God promised that He would be with Jacob wherever he went, and that He would bless him and take care of him. Now remember, Jacob had sinned. He cheated his own brother, Esau, out of his inheritance and, along with his mother, deceived his father in the process. We rightly might wonder why God would promise these things to Jacob after he sinned the way he did, but beautifully, God promises the same things to us. No matter who we are or what we have done, it is God's very nature to take care of us. The Lord has promised that He will never leave us or forsake us. God's keeping power holds us in every situation. Even when we are not tuned in to God, He is tuned in to us. God wants to bless us; even though we don't deserve it, He is committed to us.

God Will Keep Us as the Apple of His Eye

King David poetically shared this prayer to God in Psalm 17:8: "Keep me as the apple of Your eye; hide me under the shadow of Your wings." Why did King David ask God to keep him as the apple of His eye? What does this mean? The apple of an eye is the centerpiece, so to speak—the sensitive part of the eye that needs to be protected. What David is saying here is that God is sensitive toward us. He cares for us, and we are His centerpiece—His special creation.

Sometimes we blame God for the happenings in our lives—or we believe that He doesn't understand our situation or care about our feelings—but that is far from the truth. The Lord looks upon us as a father lovingly looks upon his child. God shares with the hearts of His children: "Listen, nothing is going to touch you. I have a heart toward you. I will keep you as the apple of My eye. You don't think the details are important to Me, but they are."

It was a struggle being away from my church for eight months. I spent a lot of time asking myself, *What if the people in my church leave? What about my leaders? I haven't been available for them as I should.* I had to trust these details and many others to God's hand. It was a struggle to believe that there was good that would come from my being in the hospital for eight months. It was a struggle for my wife to experience yet another season in life during which I was laid up.

The key for me then was the same as it is for all of us in our difficulties: We must take one day at a time, constantly choosing to believe with all our heart that the Lord makes everything beautiful in His time (see Eccles. 3:11). Scripture tells us that "all things work together for good" for those who are called by His name (see Rom. 8:28). When I was going through my long trial, the Lord gave me specific Scriptures for blessing and strength, like Psalm 84:11, which promises, "For the Lord God is a sun and shield; the Lord will give grace and glory; no good thing will He withhold from those who walk uprightly."

Another verse God gave me, specifically for the pain I was enduring, was Psalm 119:71, which says, "It is good for me that I have been afflicted, that I may learn Your statutes." I remember reading this Scripture verse and thinking, *Lord, did I hear You right—I need to be afflicted in order to learn something? What if I try listening a little better next time?* Finally, the Lord drew my attention to Psalm 73:28, which says, "But it is good for me to draw near to God; I have put my trust in the Lord God, that I may declare all Your works."

It was absolutely critical for me to draw closer to the Lord during this season; as I did, I realized that if I was seeking Him, He would never take my church or my wife away from me. In fact, just as He did for Job, He would give me everything back and then some! God works in all areas of our lives and does not miss one thing—not one detail gets by Him. Because God is sovereignly in control, all the details of our lives have a way of working out for His glory and for our blessing. We matter to God. His power keeps us as the apple of His eye.

God Will Keep Us in His Pavilion

Psalm 31:20 expresses the psalmist's gratefulness to God: "You shall hide them in the secret place of Your presence from the plots of man; You shall keep them secretly in a pavilion from the strife of tongues." It's not necessary to go up into the mountains to get right with God. We don't even have to leave our house. The presence of God is in us, around us, under us, before us and for us at all times. When people come against us, God's presence hides us and serves as our shelter.

Do you ever yearn for a hiding place away from the troubles, away from the difficult people, and away from your own heartaches? God serves as our shelter. His presence wraps around us and shields us from the day-to-day situations that can rob us of His joy. In fact, the Bible tells us that in His presence is the fullness of joy (see Ps. 16:11).

Are you overwhelmed? Cry out to God and say, "Bring me close to Your heart, Lord, and hide me in Your shelter, for I am discouraged and overwhelmed."

He will respond, "You have a secret place to hide right here, right now, and that is in My presence."

God Will Keep Us in His Perfect Peace

These marvelous verses from Scripture should encourage all of us:

> Be anxious for nothing, but in everything by prayer and supplication, with thanksgiving, let your requests be made known to God; and the peace of God, which surpasses all understanding, will guard your hearts and minds through Christ Jesus (Phil. 4:6-7).

Just as God keeps our hearts in Him by His power, He will also keep our minds steadfast and at peace. In other words, our minds do not have to run amok with chaotic thoughts and paranoia. The Bible tells us that "God has not given us a spirit of fear, but of power and of love and of a sound mind" (2 Tim. 1:7). We don't have to become paranoid. We don't have to read into things or blow things out of proportion. We don't have to think the worst. Instead, we should allow God to heal our minds with the blood of Jesus Christ.

How do we do this? The Bible declares that we can bring every thought under the captivity of the Spirit (see 2 Cor. 10:5). In other words, when a thought comes into your mind and stirs up anxiety or fear, you can stop it from going any further by the Spirit of God. God's power will help you rein in your thoughts and bring them together so they don't multiply like crazy. Isaiah 26:3 shares a beautiful promise: "You will keep him in perfect peace, whose mind is stayed on You, because he trusts in You."

No matter what we go through or experience, when we focus on the Lord and keep our minds on Him, we will enjoy perfect peace—a peace that trusts God and is calm in the midst of tribulation.

God Will Keep Us Persevering by His Great Power

The apostle Peter defined another way we are kept by God when he described the readers of his first epistle as those "who are kept by the power of God through faith for salvation ready to be revealed in the last time" (1 Pet. 1:5). What makes us persevere in the faith? Is it our own strength? No, we can't keep ourselves going. It is the power of God Himself, who keeps us on the path and holds us up. When we're ready to give up, God gives us the strength to hang on. It is God's power that overwhelms us and enables us to do what's right. Most importantly, it is God's power that keeps us in Him to the very end. When you've trusted in Him, your salvation is secure. You can't lose it. When you accept Jesus Christ into your heart, your name is written in the Book of Life. God will make sure that you do indeed cross that finish line into eternal life with Him.

God Will Keep Us from the Evil One

Before Jesus went to the cross, He prayed a beautiful prayer for all believers—both those who were already surrounding Him and those who would come to know Him in the ages ahead: "I have given them Your word; and the world has hated them because they are not of the world, just as I am not of the world. I do not pray that You should take them out of the world, but that You should keep them from the evil one" (John 17:14-15). Life can get rough for Christians. It can be difficult and challenging. But God has given us power to overcome the temptations, trials and discouragement we face.

Notice that in His prayer, Jesus does not ask His Father to take Christians out of the world (in other words, out of the mess that sin has produced in our world), but to keep them from the evil one. Although I must admit that I often would like just to be taken out of this sin-filled world, it is comforting to know that the Lord has His seal on us, and that the enemy of our souls has no power whatsoever over us.

As a Christian, you cannot be demon-possessed or controlled by Satan. There is nothing that the devil can do to you apart from God's allowance. No matter how evil our world gets, when you are a believer in Jesus Christ, the evil will not overcome, infiltrate, persuade or control you. The disciples came to know this power of God in a very real way, and we can be assured that the same power is upon us and keeping us from the evil one.

God Will Keep Us from Falling

Jude 1:24 shares the comforting promise that our great God "is able to keep you from stumbling, and to present you faultless before the presence of His glory with exceeding joy." God's power keeps us from falling away from Him. Does that mean we won't have times when we succumb to sin or when we struggle? No, it doesn't mean that. It does mean that God will make sure you finish the race of your faith. Jesus told Peter, "Satan has asked for you, that he may sift you as wheat. But I have prayed for you" (Luke 22:31-32). Now, if Jesus is praying for Peter, is it likely Peter is going to fall away? No.

The truth is, Jesus is praying for each of us. When we have had it, God is going to encourage us. When we want to quit, God will make sure that we don't. And when we are backsliding but keeping silent about our sin, God will bring us back because He's committed to us. This is a great God.

Unfortunately, we get overwhelmed by our problems because we don't talk about our great God. We talk about ourselves all the time—our problems, our woes, and all the issues we dislike. Rather than being overwhelmed with *self,* how about being overwhelmed by the greatness of our God?

God Will Keep Us by His Hand

What a gift it is that God holds our hand through our entire journey on this earth! Isaiah 42:6 says, "I, the Lord, have called You in righteousness, and will hold Your hand; I will keep You and give You as a covenant to the people, as a light to the Gentiles."

Think about that for a moment. We don't walk alone on our journey through life. We walk hand in hand with God. When we hold hands with our spouses or our girlfriends or boyfriends, we feel connected and comforted, don't we?

Well, the Creator of the universe loves you and holds your hand each step of the way on the journey from birth to death. Doesn't that bring you great comfort and assurance? He will hold your hand.

I remember visiting Korea some time ago and walking with a high-end government official who would be similar to our vice president. As we walked, he reached down and held my hand; I will admit I felt very uncomfortable. That custom was a part of their culture, but it was difficult for me to be at ease with a man holding my hand! Every time I tried to break loose, the guy just held my hand tighter. When it comes to God, however, would you like Him to take His hand off of you, or would you rather He held your hand tightly?

I challenge each of us to meditate on these eight distinct ways—as well as on the corresponding Scripture verses—in which God's power upholds and sustains us on a day-to-day basis. We must get to know this wonderful God of ours and allow Him to overwhelm us with His power. As we do, we will notice just how much our troubles will diminish.

STUDY QUESTIONS

1. What is the key to overcoming weakness, sin, temptation and weariness?
2. Satan would love to deter us in our faith and destroy our walk with the Lord. If Satan came after Jesus in the wilderness, he will surely come after us as well. When does Satan usually attack us, and how can we resist him?
3. List the eight distinct ways, illustrated in Scripture, in which God's power helps us on a daily basis.
4. How does God keep us from the evil one?

∾ PRAYER ∾

Thank You, Lord, that I am the apple of Your eye. Thank You that You hold me steady by Your righteous right hand and will never let me go. Though troubles will come in this life, I know that You will never leave me to face them by myself. Everything that I have need of is found in You. With You being for me and alongside me, we are a majority against the enemy. You alone have the power to deliver me out of all my troubles. Overwhelm me with Your power, I pray. Do a mighty work in me so You can do a mighty work through my life. Thank You that You do not faint or grow weary. Thank You that Your power is the same yesterday, today and for all of my tomorrows. Amen.

7

Overwhelmed by God's Holiness . . .

instead of the culture

Holiness vanishes when we talk about it,
but becomes gloriously conspicuous when you live it.
MATTHEW SOUTHALL BROWN, SR.

Give unto the Lord the glory due to His name;
worship the Lord in the beauty of holiness.
PSALM 29:2

When you hear the word "holiness," what comes to mind? Does it seem unattainable? Is it a word that can only describe God? When I spent eight months in and out of the hospital, one of the most impactful lessons God taught me was the importance of holiness in the life of a Christian. As believers, we can easily get complacent and start mixing our culture's practices with our Christian walk.

For example, I was watching television the other night, and God's name was used in vain. In the past, I would have given the show a couple of chances before turning the channel, but now I immediately turn the TV off or change to a different channel. Because of God's conviction on my heart regarding the call for holiness in my life, I tolerate way less than I used to.

It wasn't too long ago, though, that my tolerance level was much higher. It was my wife who would walk out of the room as soon as the Lord's name was taken in vain. I would sit there feeling like the anti-Christ, because my wife was more holy than I, and it was not my automatic reaction to get up and walk out after one instance of profanity. I came to realize that it was far easier to get right with the Lord than it was to deal with the condemnation, even just perceived, from my wife. When I would confess to her, however, she would communicate with freedom how important it was, for the sake of holiness, to be different from the culture. So I ask you, my reader, have you ever evaluated your life by examining your character or assessing the ethics that guide you on a day-to-day basis? Have you examined how "moral" your life is?

What does it mean to be holy? It means to be set apart for God—set apart to love and worship Him so that He can do something extraordinary in our lives. Sin keeps us from being what God wants us to be. Our own stubbornness often holds us back from being the great men and women God can make us. But if we have a heart for God and desire to do what is right in His eyes, the Lord will always work in us to mold, shape and transform us into the people He wants us to be.

Heading Toward the Temple

In looking at the concept of holiness, I want to focus on the words of Isaiah as found in two different passages—Isaiah chapter 6 and Isaiah chapter 35. Isaiah was a young prophet whose life literally changed in one day.

In 2 Chronicles 26, we read the story of King Uzziah, who reigned over the people of Israel for 52 years. For most of those years, Uzziah was a good king for the nation. Toward the end of his reign, however, he decided that he wanted more power over Israel. He wasn't satisfied with political power; he also wanted power over the people spiritually. So in unfaithfulness to the Lord, King Uzziah went into the private place of the temple to burn incense on the altar of incense. The high priest, along with 80 other courageous priests, followed King Uzziah and questioned him, for it was forbidden for him to be in the place where only priests were allowed. King Uzziah became angry and asserted that he was going to be in charge of the temple. At this moment, when King Uzziah was spewing anger at the priests, God intervened and caused King Uzziah to be afflicted with leprosy—a disease he suffered with until the day he died.

During this latter part of Uzziah's reign, the prophet Isaiah saw that his nation was falling apart because the king had rebelled against God and, as a result, the Lord had judged him. Isaiah was depressed and confused. The Bible tells us that the young prophet made his way toward the temple. Herein we see a crucial step in what it takes to be holy. First, we must head in the right direction. That's exactly what Isaiah did. No matter what had happened—no matter how despondent he felt—Isaiah headed toward the temple. He went to the Lord for answers and guidance. Because Isaiah displayed this heart attitude, God would use this young man mightily.

When we look throughout Scripture, we discover that those who sought the Lord—who headed toward the temple—were used by God time and again. We see an example of this in the apostles Peter and John, who were on their way to the temple when they encountered a lame man. Peter told him, "Silver and gold I do not have, but what I do have I give you: In the name of Jesus Christ of Nazareth, rise up and walk" (Acts 3:6). In their pursuit of Him, God used Peter and John to heal a man, who then jumped up and began praising God.

Consequently, when we are heading toward the temple, we are going in the right direction on our journey of faith. Sadly, people often head in the wrong direction when life becomes overwhelming. Eighty percent of people do not come to church or do not "want to be around the Lord" when difficult things happen to them. Instead of choosing this misguided reaction, we must make a firm commitment to continue walking toward the Lord—not away from Him—when the journey gets difficult, which it will.

In our world today, we all face a myriad of problems; these trials take a toll on our relationships and on our spiritual walk with the Lord. I challenge you: Don't allow the culture around you to sway you from the truth of God's Word. Make sure you are headed in the right direction—head toward the "temple" of God so that you can be overwhelmed by God's holiness and not by the ways of the world.

When We "See the Lord"

The prophet Isaiah wrote, "In the year that King Uzziah died, I saw the Lord sitting on a throne, high and lifted up, and the train of His robe filled the temple" (Isa. 6:1). Isaiah had put too much faith in King Uzziah. The king was a very powerful man, who "did what was right in the eyes of the Lord" (2 Chron. 26:4, NIV) for most of his reign, but he ultimately overstepped his God-given boundaries and was judged as a result.

Too often, we put leaders on a pedestal; then when they fail, it can have a devastating effect. It is especially disheartening when a pastor or Christian leader falls away from God. Sadly, I have watched many people walk away from God when this happens. While it is true that we are commanded to respect and hold in high esteem the leaders in our lives, we must always keep God as our primary focus.

The principle works as the apostle Paul laid it out: "Imitate me, just as I also imitate Christ" (1 Cor. 11:1). Yet Isaiah and the people of Israel had put too much faith in King Uzziah, and when he rebelled against God, they were devastated. The Lord removed Uzziah from the scene. God does this sometimes; He removes things or people out of our lives because we put too much focus on them. God wants us to understand that person or that item is dispensable.

I remember one lesson that I had to learn early on in my ministry life. It had been my dream to work at Calvary Chapel Costa Mesa under Pastor Chuck Smith. I begged, pleaded and became a squeaky wheel. Of course, God had another plan, and Chuck Smith knew it too.

One day when I went to Chuck's office, he told me about a church he wanted me to pastor. I could not believe his words—my very own church to pastor. I was excited and began to rejoice—prematurely. My bubble of excitement burst as Chuck told me that the church was in Twentynine Palms, a town in the desert of California. I thought, *There must be a mistake; I hate Twentynine Palms!* I remembered driving there frequently with my parents when I was a kid, because my two aunts lived there. I couldn't fathom why God would want to send me to such a godforsaken place as Twentynine Palms. Unfortunately, there was no mistake, and that's where I was assigned.

When I told my wife, Gail, who was pregnant with our first child, she started to cry. When we drove our U-Haul trailer up to Twentynine Palms, she cried the entire way. The first Sunday that I was to preach at the church, Gail's water broke, and I had to drive her to the hospital before I went on to the church to preach.

Years went by, and I eventually had to close down the church in Twentynine Palms. One of the hardest days of my life was when I handed the church keys to Pastor Chuck Smith. After I dropped the keys into his extended hand, Pastor Chuck just turned around and left without saying one word to me. That was my first lesson on how God can take away something we love or possess if it's necessary for our spiritual growth. It's a tough—but vital—lesson to learn: God must be the focus of our faith and the foundation of our lives.

So it was that the Lord God had removed King Uzziah from the throne. At this time, Isaiah headed to the temple and in essence beseeched the Lord with the query, "Lord, the throne is empty. What are we to do?" In response, God told Isaiah to look up—and when Isaiah looked up, he saw the Lord. The place was filled with the glory

111

of God! Although the circumstances of his outer world were falling apart, Isaiah saw the Lord; now everything was in perfect order.

Isaiah's experience of having his perspective change when he saw the Lord was not unique. Daniel saw the Lord and fell to the dirt in worship. Job said that when he saw God, he fell down and began to worship Him. In Revelation 1:17, John relates that when he saw the Lord, he fell at His feet as though he were dead. Bottom line, seeing God rocks a person.

To summarize what we've discussed: In order to be holy, we must be moving in the right direction; plus it's imperative to see the Lord. By ourselves, we are unable to come to a position of holiness. Some of us think we can, but we can't. We can study all we want, pray all we want and do everything in our power to obey, but we will still be unable to attain our goal. However, when we see God, everything changes—our perspective, our attitude and our behavior. Isaiah saw the Lord lifted up, with His glory filling the temple, and that transformed his view of the difficult circumstances with which he was contending.

Often our problem is that we don't see the Lord. In fact, we take notice of everything but the Lord. We regard our problems, other people and our fleshly desires, but we don't behold the Lord. When this is the case, all these other things take precedence over our relationship with God. But when all of a sudden we stop and catch sight of God, then He changes our priorities. Temporal things that once appeared so important become trivial compared to God's work in our lives.

Facing God's Holiness: When We Realize "I Am Undone . . ."

Another thing that happens when we "see the Lord" is a realization of our own sinfulness. When faced with a holy God, we become conscious of just how far short of God's standard of perfection we fall.

Let's look at Isaiah's initial reaction to seeing God:

Above it stood seraphim; each one had six wings: with two he covered his face, with two he covered his feet, and with two he flew. And one cried to another and said: "Holy, holy, holy is the Lord of hosts; the whole earth is full of His glory!" And the posts of the door were shaken by the voice of him who cried out, and the house was filled with smoke. So I said: "Woe is me, for I am undone! Because I am a man of unclean lips, and I dwell in the midst of a people of unclean lips; for my eyes have seen the King, the Lord of hosts" (Isa. 6:2-5).

In the presence of God, there's no justifying or making excuses for sin. When King David's eyes were opened by the words of Nathan the prophet, he didn't make excuses but simply said, "I have sinned against the Lord" (2 Sam. 12:13). Why do we attempt to hide our sin in the presence of God? The wise and humble way to respond to His holiness is to say honestly, "I know You are holy, Lord; I know You are great and all-knowing, and nothing is hidden from Your view. You know my heart, Lord. I'm not going to lie to You. I have sinned before You."

When we first behold God, it will feel uncomfortable. After recognizing God's greatness, His goodness and His faithfulness, we should realize that He desires another step on our part—a step of humility that leads toward holiness. Observing the cross should break our hearts because therein we comprehend that Jesus took the penalty for the sins of each one of us. As we recognize our sinfulness before a holy God, we must humble ourselves before Him and desire to be like Him—pure and holy. We understand that God is holy; after all, that's His nature and His character. So if God is holy, why would we call ourselves "Christian" but not be holy? The very nature of God is in us; therefore, we must accept that God wants us to be holy.

The apostle Peter charged, "As He who called you is holy, you also be holy in all your conduct" (1 Pet. 1:15).

Isaiah saw God and immediately understood how sinful he was before a just Lord. What about you? If you are making excuses for your sin—offering explanations for why you can't be holy—then I doubt that you have seen the Lord. Our society loves to make excuses for all the sins that people commit. Consider the following:

- Man calls sin an accident; God calls it an abomination.
- Man calls sin a blunder; God calls it blindness.
- Man calls sin a chance; God calls it a choice.
- Man calls sin a defect; God calls it a disease.
- Man calls sin an error; God calls it enmity.
- Man calls sin a fascination; God calls it a fatality.
- Man calls sin an infirmity; God calls it iniquity.
- Man calls sin a luxury; God calls it lawlessness.
- Man calls sin a mistake; God calls it madness.
- Man calls sin a trifle; God calls it a tragedy.
- Man calls sin a weakness; God calls it willfulness.

The young prophet cried out that he was undone because he was in the presence of a holy God. God was speaking to Isaiah, and when God speaks, things begin to happen. Life begins to change. Our status quo is shaken up, and we find ourselves undone. But we need not panic. Rather, we ought to rejoice because God is on the move, and He is going to do a fantastic work in our lives.

When God's Holiness Touches Us: The Removal of Our Iniquities

Consider what happens to Isaiah after he recognizes and acknowledges his sinfulness:

114

STEVE MAYS

Then one of the seraphim flew to me, having in his hand a live coal which he had taken with the tongs from the altar. And he touched my mouth with it, and said: "Behold, this has touched your lips; your iniquity is taken away, and your sin purged."

Also I heard the voice of the Lord, saying: "Whom shall I send, and who will go for Us?"

Then I said, "Here am I! Send me" (Isa. 6:6-8).

D. L. Moody once said, "There are two ways of covering our sins: man's way and God's way. If you seek to hide them, they will have a resurrection sometime. But if you let the Lord cover them, neither the devil nor man will ever be able to find them again."

Imagine Isaiah's joy when he was told that God had forgiven his sin—that his iniquity was taken away. Psalm 103:12 describes this amazing, glorious truth: "As far as the east is from the west, so far has He removed our transgressions from us." There is no blessing greater than the fact that when we confess our sins before the Lord, He forgives us and removes them, never to bring them up again (see 1 John 1:9).

What had started out as a very difficult day for Isaiah was turned around by God's touch upon him. Although he was distressed by the events going on in Israel, Isaiah sought God out by going to the temple. It was there that the young prophet beheld the Lord in His glory, confessed his sins and iniquities, and received God's forgiveness. His trajectory was instantly changed.

What about you? Have you seen the Lord? Have you humbled yourself before Him, confessing your sins and pursuing His holy touch? The Lord wants us to stop being overwhelmed by our problems and head to a place of being before God. No matter how troubled Isaiah was, he knew that the answer was to head toward the temple and to seek God.

Just as Isaiah didn't make excuses as to why he could not go to the temple, we should not make excuses for not going to church. God will honor us if we head in the right direction. Instead of staying at home and wallowing in our troubles, we must seek the Lord; instead of running away from Him, it is critical to find Him in a place of worship. When we behold God and His glory, our lives are changed because we recognize our own sinfulness and desire His touch—His forgiveness—upon our lives.

Notice what happened when Isaiah was forgiven of his sins: He was then willing to serve God. When the Lord asked, "Whom shall I send?" Isaiah responded, "Here am I! Send me" (Isa. 6:8). God saw Isaiah's heart and knew, "There's my man"—hence, Isaiah's calling as a prophet of God.

I'll take a person like that—a man or woman who has a heart for God and is willing to serve the Lord in whatever capacity presents itself—any day. That's the beginning of holiness: having a heart modeled after God. When we allow God's holiness to overwhelm us, we realize just how much of a sinner we are. As a result, we seek out the Lord's forgiveness—and then we are able to be used by Him.

So, I ask you: Are you upset, discouraged or despondent today? If so, take the first step and head to church to seek God. If you humble yourself and soften your heart before Him, the Lord will open your eyes. You will see the King of glory and will hear His voice. Your perspective and direction will change, and you will have a vision for what God can do through you.

Why Desire Holiness?

Why should we want a holy life? Let's explore together four reasons why holiness is a character trait to pursue.

Holiness Brings Restoration

The first reason is that the Lord's holiness brings restoration. If we *really* embrace God, He is going to restore the parts of our lives that are broken. A church attender might say to me, "Well, Pastor Steve, I need to be restored. My life is a mess; my marriage is falling apart; and I'm not happy with where I'm at in most other areas. I've been to churches and I've read books, but that hasn't worked." My response would be that all of that won't work. True restoration is a supernatural work of God. It's not something a person can generate on his or her own. Beholding the Lord and His glory and wholeheartedly following Him are what allow His Holy Spirit to touch a life, restoring "the years that the swarming locust has eaten" (Joel 2:25).

Consider these descriptive verses from the book of Isaiah:

> The wilderness and the wasteland shall be glad for them, and the desert shall rejoice and blossom as the rose; it shall blossom abundantly and rejoice, even with joy and singing. The glory of Lebanon shall be given to it, the excellence of Carmel and Sharon. They shall see the glory of the Lord, the excellency of our God (Isa. 35:1-2).

In these verses, we read that the wilderness will be glad and the desert will rejoice and blossom as a rose. Perhaps you are in a wilderness experience right now. If so, then rejoice, for your journey through the wilderness is going to lead you to a place of gladness. God is going to use your dark and painful trials to bring about His good purposes for you. Your desert experience is going to give birth to a blossoming rose. In other words, God is going to use this season to restore you, as only He can.

My recent series of hospital stays was definitely a desert experience, but it was also a time in which God brought about some miraculous restoration in my life. These words from the book of

Zephaniah were comforting and special to me: "The Lord your God in your midst, the Mighty One, will save; He will rejoice over you with gladness, He will quiet you with His love, He will rejoice over you with singing" (Zeph. 3:17).

No doubt many of us have been lonely in the middle of the night. If we call on Him, the Lord will come and sing over us. I know that I had that experience—waking up in the middle of the night in a hospital room and feeling all alone. My wife and the doctors and nurses did the best they could. But it was the Lord who truly comforted me—especially in those dark hours when I lay awake in my hospital bed feeling lonely and deeply discouraged.

As we pursue Him, the Lord is faithful to take our wilderness experiences—times when nothing makes sense and so much is painful—and make them times of gladness. He will take the parched seasons of our lives and turn them into places of rejoicing.

Those verses in Isaiah also say that our barrenness will be turned into a place of abundance. Sometimes we feel empty, as if we just don't have anything left in us.

Have you ever felt that way? Have you ever expressed these thoughts to the Lord? "God, look at what I am going through! Why are things such a mess in my life? Why are You allowing this to happen to me?"

If you have asked those honest questions, I can assure you that the Lord wants to communicate to you: "When I get done with My work in this season, you will find joy and will rejoice in your heart and not be bitter. Let Me complete My good work in you at this time."

Only God can take the wilderness and desert experiences and make them times of rejoicing. Only the Lord can bring abundance out of barrenness. So what is our role during this process? It is simply to seek God, allowing ourselves to be overwhelmed by His holiness and not giving bitterness permission to take root.

Sometimes, though, we don't get rid of bitterness. For example, perhaps after a rough patch in our marriage, we begin to figure out our spouse, and our relationship smoothes out—but we don't get rid of some long-standing resentment. Maybe we hold on to some hurt from earlier years in our lives, and that ruins everything God is building now. Or we might let the kids back into the home, but we're still angry at them. Sometimes we get upset about certain issues in our church and won't let that go, so we're not fed in the way God wants us to be.

When God begins His restorative work in your life, that means He's making you brand new. It means that your wilderness is now joy, your desert is now rejoicing, and your barrenness is now abundance. God does what seems to be impossible in our lives.

When God's holiness fills us, the glory of the Lord will cover us. Even in the most challenging circumstances, God will make that very situation, no matter how ugly it may seem, into a thing of beauty. Really? Yes, really. When God is working in the midst of a problem, it becomes an object of beauty as He uses it to mold us into His likeness.

Basically, when God restores us, He brings fruitfulness. No longer are we barren, because we have seen God and have been touched by God; like Isaiah, we will never be the same. God wipes away that barrenness and uses us in a mighty way. The prophet Isaiah saw the Lord, was touched by the Lord, and heard the Lord's voice; then he responded, "Here am I! Send me." God used this young man mightily, and Isaiah was never the same. After this powerful calling, he went on to become one of the most prominent Old Testament prophets.

When God touches a person, the heart is changed. Haven't we all come across people who try to restore themselves or use motivational programs to bring about change? The problem with these programs is that they don't change the heart. They don't bring about the godly change that only the Lord can accomplish. The program might help with some outward differences, but it doesn't transform the heart. It might give a person a position, but it doesn't change the internal desire. If we want to be all we were created to be, then we must let God restore us. Turning toward holiness allows God to do His work of restoration.

Holiness Brings Redemption

Second, God's holiness brings redemption. Let's think about this for a moment. If God is the only One who can restore a life, then He's also the only One who can redeem. We read in Isaiah 35:3-4, "Strengthen the weak hands, and make firm the feeble knees. Say to those who are fearful-hearted, 'Be strong, do not fear! Behold, your God will come with vengeance, with the recompense of God; He will come and save you.'"

Other people can pick us up and serve or assist us, but only God can perform a complete fix. These verses speak of God redeeming our hands. Men can become exhausted after laboring for 20 or 30 years, so they give up. Figuratively speaking, their hands are tired; they're weak and feeble. God will strengthen those hands and put them back in the battle. He will energize the weary person to lift up holy hands before the Lord.

In the same verse, we also read that God will redeem our knees. What on earth does this mean? In the book of Ezekiel, the prophet talks about the water of the Holy Spirit grabbing the knees (see Ezek. 47:4), which means that God has a person's prayer life in His hands. God teaches us how to pray through His Holy Spirit and empowers us to have a strong prayer life.

Finally, God redeems people's hearts. Consider some sources of fearful-heartedness: Are you afraid of losing your home? Are you afraid of getting laid off or fired? Are you afraid that you will never get married? Are you afraid that your marriage is headed toward divorce? Are you afraid your children will become prodigals? God says you are to be strong and not fear, because He is going to come and save you.

As we seek after His holiness, God is committed to restoring and redeeming us. But it's vital to remember: If we don't run after holiness—if we don't choose to be set apart for the Lord—then we will not experience God's power in our lives. Holiness is not a word to run from. It's a vital part of living the Christian life—of following God. Just as He is holy, so shall we be. When we see the Lord, He touches our lives and takes us down that highway of holiness. Rather than resisting what God is doing, we should fully embrace His work and excitedly watch how He makes everything beautiful in His time.

Holiness Brings Revival

Third, God's holiness brings revival in our lives. As we continue reading in Isaiah, the prophet writes:

> Then the eyes of the blind shall be opened, and the ears of the deaf shall be unstopped. Then the lame shall leap like a deer, and the tongue of the dumb sing. For waters shall burst forth in the wilderness, and streams in the desert. The parched ground shall become a pool, and the thirsty land springs of water; in the habitation of jackals, where each lay, there shall be grass with reeds and rushes (Isa. 35:5-7).

Sometimes we're blind to things happening around us and to what God is doing in our lives. But then God opens our eyes in a spiritual sense, and we truly see and understand. At other times we're deaf—we don't hear the voice of God speaking to us. Someone might say to me, "Pastor Steve, I haven't heard the Spirit for years."

I would respond, "Why do you think that is? Do you want to be holy? Do you want to do what God tells you to do?"

I might hear back, "No. I don't want to do the hard work; I want to go only so far in my Christian life, and that's it."

The Christian walk doesn't work that way. Ninety-nine percent of obedience is a head-on collision between God's way and our way. He wants it all. God created us, bought us, and made us His people. He chose us and rescued us out of the pit; He wants us set apart for Him so He can make us into a work of art. The Lord has a clear vision for what He plans to do, but often we resist His work of doing it. All of our sin exists within His clear view—when a person is sleeping with someone to whom they are not married; all the shady business deals a person is doing under the table; the addictions to substances or destructive behaviors; the double standard a person is living, perhaps on the outside portraying a great Christian guy or gal while seeking out pornography or alcohol when no one is looking. The list of sins is unending. These sins, and multiple others, are unholy and unethical.

Bottom line, who we truly are is manifested when no one is around—when we think no one is looking. God, however, is omniscient, meaning He has full knowledge of and sees everything. God the Spirit might be beckoning our hearts with the simple question: "Do you like who you are when no one is watching?" If the answer is no, God can and will change us—if we allow Him to through our complete surrender.

He may have to orchestrate a difficult situation in order to bring about His wonderful work of restoration, redemption and revival. Instead of being overwhelmed by these difficult circumstances and resisting God, we must surrender to Him and allow Him to do His work. If we give Him that access and freedom, we will find that He will restore us like no one else can.

If we allow Him to work, we will find that He will redeem our hearts, our hands and our knees. He will redeem our spiritual walk with Him so that we are on the path of holiness. He will revive us and give us a strength that we've never had before, because, in spiritual senses, our eyes are going to see and our ears are going to hear and our feet are going to run. The dry and parched areas will turn into overflowing pools. Let me ask, "Can anyone besides God do that?"

Holiness Brings Renewal

Finally, we should pursue holiness because it brings renewal in our lives. Perhaps we can be humble enough to say, "Okay, God, if this is what holiness really is—allowing You to work in my life—and all I have to do is get on the highway and go God's way . . . well, I want to do that!" We read in Isaiah 35:8-10:

> A highway shall be there, and a road, and it shall be called the Highway of Holiness. The unclean shall not pass over it, but it shall be for others. Whoever walks the road, although a fool, shall not go astray. No lion shall be there, nor shall any ravenous beast go up on it; it shall not be found there. But the redeemed shall walk there, and the ransomed of the Lord shall return, and come to Zion with singing, with everlasting joy on their heads. They shall obtain joy and gladness, and sorrow and sighing shall flee away.

In other words, for the redeemed, there are not going to be any obstacles. Often obstacles rear up throughout our lives. But with God we're going to be able to walk down this highway with nothing standing in the way of His work in our lives. We are going to be redeemed.

Now there is a low road—that low road is the way of Satan. That is for those who erringly reject God's redemption. Trust me, we cannot think we are going to heaven but at the same time reject God's redemption and His holiness in our lives. It's a glorious truth that when we see God, He never leaves us in the same state; He changes us and molds us into His image.

The process begins with being born again. When a person is born again, his eyes will see the Lord and his ears will hear what God is saying. God is in the business of renewal. He will breathe new hope into a discouraging situation. He will renew a person's strength in the face of difficult experiences. He will re-create a life. The Christian life is not easy, with its temptations to resist and godly choices to make, but there will never be anyone like God in our lives, because He is the only One who can restore, redeem, revive and renew a person.

Therefore, I challenge each of us: We cannot allow ourselves to be overwhelmed by the way of culture. We must choose the highway of holiness—that is, heading in the right direction and seeking the Lord. When we allow ourselves to be overwhelmed by God's holiness, we will experience joy and peace in the midst of our wilderness and desert experiences. The beautiful hope and promise is that the Lord will not leave us in the arid places but will replace our barrenness with abundance and the ugliness of our situation with the beauty of His power and glory.

STUDY QUESTIONS

1. When we look up and "see the Lord," what happens?
2. When we come face to face with God's holiness, what do we realize?
3. What happens when God's holiness touches us?
4. List and examine the four reasons we should pursue holiness in our lives.

∽ PRAYER ∽

Lord, I don't want to resist Your work. I want to stop running my own life and turn toward You. I want Your goodness and holiness to transform and renew me. I surrender to You right now. Overwhelm me with Your holiness and mold me and make me into Your image, I pray. Amen.

8

Overwhelmed by God's Spirit . . .

instead of the direction of men and the culture

You might as well try to hear without ears or breathe without lungs,
as to try to live a Christian life without the Spirit of God in your heart.
D. L. MOODY

I indeed baptized you with water,
but He will baptize you with the Holy Spirit.
MARK 1:8

What problem is causing you to be overwhelmed? Have you tried to fix that problem? Have you tried to repair your marriage, but to no avail? Have you tried to reform your kids, without any luck? Are you beset by a plaguing sin that you just can't seem to stand against? Furthermore, have you talked to friends, family and counselors in search of an answer to your problem—only to find that those resources haven't worked either?

We read in Zechariah 4:6, "This is the word of the Lord to Zerubbabel: 'Not by might nor by power, but by My Spirit,' says the Lord of hosts." As this verse attests, we cannot fix our problems by our own strength or ingenuity. The "fix" for the problems we

125

face—physical issues, relational and marital issues, even economic issues—must be a work of the Holy Spirit. The Holy Spirit carries out God's will in a believer's life, and it is by the indwelling power of God's Spirit that relationships are restored and problems are brought to an unexpected end.

The Lord is in the business of changing lives. Often, as part of that process, He allows difficult circumstances to enter our lives in order to fashion us into the godly people He wants us to be. Through trials and difficulties, God is able to draw us into a much deeper walk with Him. Furthermore, it is by His Spirit that He works out all things for good according to His purposes.

We humans frequently attempt to "fix" our own problems. If that doesn't work, we look to other people for answers. Instead, we should cultivate the discipline of looking to God first in all circumstances. Acts 1:8 reminds us that it is God's Spirit who will give power and guidance when we are overwhelmed: "But you shall receive power when the Holy Spirit has come upon you; and you shall be witnesses to Me in Jerusalem, and in all Judea and Samaria, and to the end of the earth." Moreover, the Spirit of the living God can heal people physically, can save marriages, can protect children, and can intervene in life circumstances to bring about God's will and transformation. Once we understand what is necessary—and surrender to the work of the Holy Spirit to bring about transformation—God moves in amazing ways.

Too often, we focus on temporal problems rather than on our relationship with the Lord. At other times, we treat God like a genie, wanting Him to give us "power" or "quick fixes" to overcome health, sin or relational issues.

God does not dispense power to humans for use as a tool. Power alone corrupts. Consider the governments and leaders of the world and how their power is often corrupted. Human beings cannot handle power without having restraints and boundaries.

Too often, we believers make demands of the Holy Spirit: "I want power to manage this lust. I want power not to commit adultery against my spouse. I want power to change my attitude." It sounds ridiculous, doesn't it? God doesn't just dole out the "power wand" to us whenever we ask. Why? We don't need power in and of itself. Rather, God empowers us differently: He calls us to be in complete submission to the Holy Spirit so that He can work through us to give us the ability to do what's right and to conform to His will.

The Holy Spirit's Role

The Holy Spirit is a person—the third member of the Trinity. The apostle John, by recording the words of Jesus, gave us access to some key truths about the Spirit, who lives in our hearts and gives us the help necessary to live the Christian life of faith. At one point, Jesus told His disciples, "Nevertheless I tell you the truth. It is to your advantage that I go away; for if I do not go away, the Helper will not come to you; but if I depart, I will send Him to you" (John 16:7). On another occasion, He said, "But the Helper, the Holy Spirit, whom the Father will send in My name, He will teach you all things, and bring to your remembrance all things that I said to you" (John 14:26). When we open our mouths, the Spirit gives us words to speak. When strength is necessary, as our Helper, He provides it.

After receiving the Holy Spirit into our hearts and understanding that He wants to live there like Christ, we realize that the Holy Spirit is our power. We don't have to beg for power; we just have to ask the Holy Spirit to teach and lead us. One of His main purposes is to bring us closer to Christ—to teach us everything we need to know about the Lord and to empower us to live according to His Word. But what do we sometimes do? We resist the Holy Spirit—or quench His work by choosing to live in our flesh. Then we wonder why we have problems and why we are overwhelmed! Bottom line, it is vitally important to stop saying no to the Holy Spirit and instead choose to yield to Him.

During World War II, Winston Churchill delivered many prominent speeches. In one of his more famous speeches, he declared boldly, "We shall defend our island, whatever the cost may be. We shall fight on the beaches, we shall fight on the landing grounds, we shall fight in the fields and in the streets, we shall fight in the hills; we shall never surrender." After speaking these bold and courageous words, however, he went off the air, burst into tears, and fell over his desk in despair. "We will never give up," he later said to his leaders. "We will fight them with everything we have, but we have nothing except beer bottles to fight them with."

He then sent a message to the president of the United States, which ended with, "Give us the tools, and we will finish the job." His point: "We can take Hitler out—we can stop this thing—but we are out of bullets and we have no weapons. We have no planes and we are almost dead, but if you will just give us the basic things we need, we can finish this and knock him all the way off the map." The United States did help Britain; as we all know, the two countries joined forces to stop Hitler and Nazi Germany in their tracks.

I can't help but believe that sometimes we are saying very similar things to God as Churchill said to his leaders. We are exhausted, but we don't want to quit. We want to do right and prevail against our enemy, but we're out of ammunition and feel about ready to die. So we ask God to give us power—to give us what is necessary to accomplish the job. And God answers, "I already did. I baptized you in the Holy Spirit, but you are not looking to Him for your help!"

Therein lies the key problem: We often do not rely on the Holy Spirit. We don't look to Him for our peace, our strength and our sustenance. Trying to live the Christian life on our own simply does not work. Another role of the Holy Spirit is to help us function in this world. Sadly, we often resist Him and reject the gifts of the Spirit—the very means that enable us to follow and serve the Lord.

Instead, a believer should humbly pray, "Holy Spirit, please give me everything I need to walk in a manner worthy of God's name. I ask You to give me self-control, wisdom, knowledge, discernment and all the fruits of the Spirit." When a prayer such as this is offered to Him, God will honor the heartfelt request and use this servant in a mighty way in his or her home, job, church and community.

In contrast to this humble reliance on the Spirit is the abundance of schisms and tension in churches because the Holy Spirit is being thrown out. A. W. Tozer related this concept best: "If the Holy Spirit was withdrawn from the church today, 95 percent of what we do would go on and no one would know the difference." Isn't that a sad truth? Instead of relying on the Holy Spirit, we are relying on our committees, boards, pastors, elders and the congregation itself. Truly, apart from God and the working of His Spirit in our lives, we can do nothing.

Because many Christians are not relying on the Holy Spirit, our witness is lacking. Our light is dim—as opposed to the big shining torch that we should be in our homes, with our friends and in our community. The Spirit of God should so shine in us that people can't help but behold the glory of God in our lives. The Spirit of God needs to come upon us that way. People should easily detect that we are on fire for God. However, because we resist the Holy Spirit, the fire and passion are quenched, and people do not perceive the joy of the Lord. What do they see instead? They observe a defeated Christian who is overwhelmed by everything but the power of the Holy Spirit!

I've heard a story about a certain guide who lived in the deserts of Arabia and never lost his way. He carried with him a homing pigeon that had a very fine cord attached to one of its legs. When in doubt as to which path to take, the guide would throw the bird into the air. The pigeon quickly strained at the cord to fly in the direction of home—and thus led the guide accurately toward his destination. Because of this unique practice, he was known as the "dove man." In a similar fashion, the Holy Spirit, our heavenly Dove, willingly and ably directs us on the narrow way that leads to the more abundant life—if in humble self-denial, we submit to His unerring supervision.

The Early Church (Christians): Relying on the Holy Spirit

The Early Church was filled with believers who were on fire for God. Although they faced persecution, these disciples were able to spread the gospel because they relied on the Holy Spirit. They had incredible faith, knowing that their God could do anything.

Their God Was Able to Give Life

The early believers knew that their God was able to give life. As we read in the book of Acts, they saw Dorcas, a disciple who lived in Joppa, raised from the dead (see Acts 9:36-42). They witnessed people being healed. They knew that God was a miracle-working God. It wasn't only physical lives to which He gave life and healing; the Lord also gave spiritual life to the Church. The Early Church grew not because of money, great programs or rock-star pastors, but by a supernatural work of the Holy Spirit. The Holy Spirit brought thousands of people at a time to a saving knowledge of Jesus, and churches were literally established overnight. The principle we must understand here is that it's God who brings people to Himself.

The faith of the Early Church was strong because of the power of the Holy Spirit manifested through them. In one instance, Peter and John ministered to a lame man outside the temple. The man asked for money; Peter, knowing there was a better gift, responded,

"Silver and gold I do not have, but what I do have I give you: In the name of Jesus Christ of Nazareth, rise up and walk" (Acts 3:6). The Early Church believers were poor in resources but rich in fellowship; they shared everything they did have. But truly they possessed what was most important: They had the power of the Holy Spirit leading them and working through them. They knew that they could do all things through Him.

It is crucially important for us to understand the life-changing power of the Holy Spirit. Before the Holy Spirit was given to him, Peter denied Jesus Christ in a mindset of fear, but after the Holy Spirit came upon him, Peter courageously preached the gospel and healed people. Before the Holy Spirit, Saul (Paul) was murdering Christians, but after he received the Holy Spirit and became a new man, Paul was a missionary sold out for the gospel of Jesus Christ. That is the transformative power of the Spirit at work. The early believers understood this truth. They clung to the Lord and relied on the baptism of the Holy Spirit not only to live the Christian life, but also to serve God and bring Him glory.

By the way, it's not just the pastor who is meant to have this kind of faith. Whether a child or a senior of 99 years, we are all called to have great faith in God and to rely on the Holy Spirit to serve God and do great things for His kingdom. The early Christians witnessed, on a regular basis, the power of the Holy Spirit to raise people from the dead, to heal the lame, and to give sight to the blind. They relied on God to give life not only to those who were sick or dying, but also to the Church.

Their God Was Able to Touch Them

God's presence was tangibly real to the early believers. Of course, His original disciples and many of the early converts had actually been in Jesus' company while He walked on earth. They had enjoyed eating with Him, conversing with Him, and resting with Him.

Jesus had touched them in an authentic and undeniable way. When He called them, they left everything behind to follow the Lord. These men and women who walked the earth with Jesus certainly yielded to Him. However, many also came to believe in Jesus through the testimony of the apostles and the Early Church members. The Holy Spirit was palpably alive to these early believers. They yielded to Him and were touched by Him. The book of Acts, the book of Romans and the other New Testament epistles contain plentiful examples of how the touch of God energized the Early Church.

It's important to remember that the Christians of the Early Church did not have an easy existence. We might be tempted to think that it was simpler to be a Christian then, when the eyewitnesses were still alive—when the original apostles were sharing what they had seen and heard when Jesus walked the earth.

But the reality is that we have it much easier as believers in our day and age. We have the completed canon of Scripture available at our fingertips as well as countless theological commentaries, Bible study resources and Christian literature. We have huge churches that provide numerous opportunities to learn about the Lord and to fellowship with other believers; and, for the most part, at least in some countries, we have the freedom to worship and believe without being persecuted. The Early Church did not have any of these resources, and first-century believers suffered intense persecution and chastisement for their faith in Christ. Yet these early Christians were on fire. They were sold out to Christ and yielded to the Holy Spirit. God directed their steps and added to the Church on a daily basis.

Their God Was Able to Change Them

One of the biggest testimonies about Christianity is the witness of "changed lives." No other religion in the world can show a miracle of changed lives comparable to what happens when people come to know and follow Jesus Christ. The Early Church turned the world up-side down because God so radically changed people's lives. Murderers became self-sacrificing leaders. Idolaters became faithful follow-ers of Christ. Rough fishermen became compassionate theologians. Cowards became courageous individuals. The weak became strong. The insecure became bold. Hostile crowds became congregations. And all of them together became instruments of the Holy Spirit to change the world for God.

Their God Was Able to Use Them

The early believers were used mightily by God to spread the gospel. They were dedicated to the Lord and yielded to His Holy Spirit. In the face of painful persecution and trials, they did not quit, nor did they complain. Their light burned bright until it was extinguished by death. In fact, many of the apostles and early believers died as martyrs for their belief in Christ.

Another reason the Early Church was so effective is that the Christians of that day genuinely cared about one another. They were a united body of believers—often living communally and sharing all they owned, not only with the local church in their area but also with other fellowships in other regions. The Early Church was permeated with the love of God. He held preeminence in the believers' lives, and they yielded to the Holy Spirit, who directed their every move. That's why the Church bore so much fruit, regardless of how much persecu-tion the believers had to endure. I like what R. Kent Hughes says about the Holy Spirit working in the Church:

- Where the Spirit reigns, believers relate to the Word—teaching.
- Where the Spirit reigns, believers relate to each other—koinonia.
- Where the Spirit reigns, believers relate to God—worship.
- Where the Spirit reigns, believers relate to the world—evangelism.

The Church (Christians) Today: Are We Neglecting the Holy Spirit?

When we marvel over the wonderful model of the Early Church and its sold-out believers, we have to ask, "Is the Church like this today?" Our answer is likely that, overall, the Church today seems to lack the fire and the commitment to God that the Early Church possessed. The next logical question would be, "Why is that?" Let's examine three ways in which the Church today is misguided.

We Have Lost Our Identity

What does it mean to be a Christian? What is the identity of a believer? Back in the Early Church, there was a clear distinction between a believer and a nonbeliever. Sadly, in today's world, such a vivid contrast is missing. The term "user-friendly church" has become popular. Essentially what this descriptor means is that this type of church does not want to get anyone angry, to ruffle any feathers or to offend anyone; in short, it's a church that shies away from talking about sin.

So where is the contrast with the world? What makes the user-friendly church any different from the culture around it? In actuality, this church is not different; it is just like the world—and therein lies the problem. A church should undoubtedly look different from the world, with a clear distinction between the beliefs and values of the church and the beliefs and values of the world. They should not look the same. A church that is separated out to God and not sold out to the world is necessary. How can we turn our world upside down if we are actually embracing it as it is?

If all were right in our churches today, we would be so influenced and controlled by the Holy Spirit that the world would take notice. There is a great verse in the Bible that describes a man being infused by the power of the Holy Spirit: "Then the hand of the Lord came upon Elijah; and he girded up his loins and ran ahead of Ahab to the entrance of Jezreel" (1 Kings 18:46). Ahab was riding in his chariot; imagine the horses not being able to keep up with Elijah as he ran. Now that's a man operating in the power of the Holy Spirit!

That's how it should be in the Church today—we ought to have "the hand of the Lord" upon us. The Holy Spirit's power in us should cause the world to see the radical difference and desire to share in our experience of God's work. But the opposite is true: Instead of the Church influencing the world, the world (culture) is influencing the Church. When there is no notable difference between a believer and a nonbeliever, we have lost our identity and the conviction of sin.

A Spirit-filled and Spirit-led believer will stand out from the world. The values of that person will be far different from those of the culture. For one example among the many we could mention, the culture calls having sex before marriage good and beneficial, but the Christian who is yielded to the Holy Spirit claims, "No, sex is reserved for the marriage union only."

The Church today must embrace its identity in Jesus Christ. Like the Early Church, we should be so committed to Christ and so yielded to the Holy Spirit that there is a clear distinction between a believer and a nonbeliever. Ultimately, what's critical is turning our world upside down instead of being no different from it.

We Have Lost Our Power and Purpose

Here's a question to reflect on: If the Church has lost its identity—and by extension its power and its purpose—then what good are we in the world? Have we become just another social institution trying to do "good" deeds? The Bible tells us that we are to be the light of the world and the salt of the earth (see Matt. 5:13-16); if we lose our light and saltiness, how will we light up and "flavor" the world? In other words, how can we bring people to the Lord if we ourselves have lost sight of Him as the One we worship and follow?

What is the purpose of the local church? This may be a surprise, but it's not to preach the gospel. The purpose of the local church is to equip, build up and encourage believers to walk with the Lord so that they can go out and evangelize and turn their world upside down. This doesn't mean that pastors shouldn't preach the gospel or have evangelistic events at their churches, but the primary focus should be to teach and equip believers to know Christ and make Him known.

Churches should be focusing on teaching the Word of God. So many churches, however, don't even give credence to the authority of God's Word. Is it any wonder that the Body of Christ is so weak and ineffective in our world today? After His resurrection, Jesus asked Peter, "Do you love Me?" Peter answered, "Yes, Lord." Jesus responded to Peter by saying, "Then feed My sheep." Three times, Jesus asked the same question of Peter (who responded in the affirmative each time), and three times He told Peter to feed His sheep (see John 21:15-17).

God wants me, as a pastor, to feed my church members by teaching them from the Scriptures and encouraging them in their relationship with the Lord. He doesn't want me to beat them over the head or get them saved every single Sunday morning. But He does want me to nourish His people with His Word so that the congregation can grow and so that each member can be used by God in his or her circles of influence. Bottom line, the purpose of the local church is to come together to worship God and to be fed by the Word of God so that we can go out into the world, love others, and make a difference in their lives.

We Have Lost Our Mission

It is my belief that many of the churches in our world today are confused about their mission. For some, social justice seems to be their sole mission. For others, pop psychology and making people feel good about themselves seem to top their mission statement. But what is the true mission of God's Church? Very simply, our mission as the Bride of Christ is to share with an unbelieving world who God is and what He has done in our hearts. That is the Great Commission and the mission of our lives as well.

The mission statement at our church is very simple and spells out the word W-I-S-E. First, as a member of our church, I am to **W**in somebody to Jesus Christ; second, I am to **I**nstruct somebody for God; third, I am to **S**end somebody for the Lord; and fourth, I am to **E**ncourage somebody for God. What if we all lived out this mission statement every day? Might we see that there is nothing God can't do through us?

I challenge you to fulfill your God-given mission, through the power of His Spirit, in your home, job and relationships—and then watch how the Lord changes you as well as the people around you.

In a fascinating Old Testament account, the Lord told Ezekiel to measure water that was flowing out from the Temple, illustrating God's plan of salvation (see Ezek. 47:16). As the river flowed from the Temple, as it increased in volume, it brought healing and prosperity to everything in its path. Every living thing that moved, wherever the river went, would live. God wants us to understand that the river may start out small, but it will build momentum to become a torrent of living water. It has a small beginning, but it is going to take over and absolutely dominate our lives. So if we allow God's Spirit to dwell in our hearts, all we have to do is dig down and that river will fill our hearts. According to Psalm 46:4-5, "There is a river whose streams shall make glad the city of God, The holy place of the tabernacle of the Most High. God is in the midst of her, she shall not be moved; God shall help her, just at the break of dawn." That river is Jesus Christ and He is right there to fill you all the way through.

There is an analogy here that ties this illustration of the flowing waters of life from the Temple with Jesus Christ. The Bible tells us that the water flowed underneath the door of the Temple and went down the side of the mountain until it passed the altar on the right side. The living waters of life went by the altar, the place upon which offerings such as sacrifices are made. John 19:34 tells us that when the Lord was crucified on the cross, water and blood came forth out of our Savior's side: "But one of the soldiers pierced His side with a spear, and immediately blood and water came out." Jesus said, "If anyone thirsts, let him come to Me and drink. He who believes in Me, as the Scripture has said, out of his heart will flow rivers of living water." Isaiah 55:1 says, "Everyone who thirsts, come to the waters." There is a river that is so powerful that it can deliver our soul and present us faultless before the Son of God. The Holy Spirit's leading in our life will always take us the way of the cross. So to walk in the Spirit means I am living by the cross of Christ. If you are ever led away from the cross, it is the spirit of the anti-Christ, who denies Christ's existence. The cross keeps us humble before God, and when the Lord pours out His Spirit upon us, we have to give the credit to God.

The first time Ezekiel measured the water, it went up to his ankles, signifying that he was walking in the Spirit. But notice how much of Ezekiel was not covered by the water. Then God told him to measure the water again, and this time it went up to his knees. When God has us on our knees, we are praying, giving thanks, repenting, confessing and growing in our love for Jesus.

God spoke once again to His servant to measure the water; this time the water went all the way up to Ezekiel's loins—the strongest part of a man's body. God was strengthening Ezekiel, filling him more and more with His Spirit so that he could bear fruit for the Kingdom, but you could still see half of Ezekiel's body. In other words, God had half of Ezekiel and the world had half. So God told

Ezekiel to go measure the water one more time. This time the water was flowing like a mighty river, and Ezekiel was covered up to his head, so that he had to swim rather than walk. The Spirit had taken possession of his life, and he was living and moving in the power of the Holy Spirit! The Lord wants to do the same for us.

When I look at the modern-day Church of Jesus Christ, I cry out, "God, we are in dire straits!" We have lost our identity, our power and our purpose, and our mission.

I want to encourage you, dear friend. Are you committed to the Lord and yielded to the Holy Spirit? If not, I challenge you to make that commitment—and the necessary life changes—right now. Instead of being overwhelmed by the ways of this world and the direction of the culture, let God overwhelm you with His Spirit. Just like the Early Church believers, embrace your identity in God. Be filled with the power of the Holy Spirit and live out God's purpose for your life. Finally, fulfill your mission in your home, at work, in your community and wherever the Lord sends you.

If we are committed to these principles, we can be assured that God will never quit His work in us. His plans for us are not of evil but of good, to give us an expected end of a future and hope (see Jer. 29:11).

God wants to change our lives. If we are harboring unconfessed sin, we are quenching the work of the Holy Spirit. We must confess our sin and relinquish it. We must be wholly devoted to God and completely committed to walking in His ways. This undertaking will impact our marriages and our families. If we submit our hearts wholly to the Spirit's leading, it will revolutionize our commitments to our relationships, responsibilities and service to others.

Some years ago, I heard a story about a group of pastors who were discussing the possibility of having D. L. Moody serve as a speaker at a citywide evangelistic campaign. One minister was reluctant to have Moody speak. "Why Moody?" he asked. "Does he have a monopoly on the Holy Spirit?"

139

The man's question was followed by a hushed silence.

Finally another man spoke up: "No, Moody does not have a monopoly on the Holy Spirit. But the Holy Spirit does have a monopoly on D. L. Moody." Does the Holy Spirit have a monopoly on each of us?

STUDY QUESTIONS

1. Instead of being overwhelmed by the direction of men and the culture, what does God want us to be overwhelmed with?
2. What is the role of the Holy Spirit in our lives?
3. List and describe four reasons why the Christians in the Early Church were able to spread the gospel while facing persecution.
4. The Church today seems to lack the fire and the commitment to God that the Early Church possessed. List and describe three things wrong with the Church today.

∽ PRAYER ∽

Lord, overwhelm me with Your Holy Spirit. I need Your guidance, Your direction and Your leading. I do not want to carry around unconfessed sin. I do not want to grieve You or hinder Your work within my life. Forgive me. I choose today to be on fire for Your kingdom and to be led and guided by Your Spirit, and I ask that You would use me mightily for Your glory. Monopolize my life, I pray! Amen.

9

Overwhelmed by God's Word . . .

instead of the wisdom of this world

A Bible that's falling apart usually belongs to someone who isn't.
CHARLES H. SPURGEON

Your word is a lamp to my feet and a light to my path.
PSALM 119:105

No doubt we would all agree that life can often be overwhelming and confusing. When I was in the hospital, I found myself getting overwhelmed by the hospital bed, by the doctors and nurses, by the medications I was taking and by the pain I was experiencing. But I was also overwhelmed by my marriage and the strain that my ill health was putting on my wife. I was overwhelmed by the sheer number of responsibilities that had to be shouldered by my church staff while I was out of commission. And I was overwhelmed by the reality that my health had always been a trial.

Sometimes our problems just overtake us, don't they? We get overwhelmed by our marriages—or our singleness. We get over-whelmed with trying to make ends meet on very little income; we get tired of unemployment or underemployment. Really, all the pressures, demands, responsibilities and trials of life can just begin to crush or defeat us.

We all have experienced the feeling of being overwhelmed. But when I was in the midst of this feeling at the hospital, God showed me that I had things backward. My perspective was wrong. No, it definitely wasn't fun to be in the hospital, but I was looking at all the problems of my situation instead of noticing that God was using this very situation for my good. My eyes were opened to the realization that the Lord wanted me to be overwhelmed by Him and not by my circumstances. Through this revelation, my entire perspective and attitude transformed dramatically.

Being overwhelmed by our problems benefits nothing. Furthermore, being bitter, resentful or cynical eventually will bring personal destruction and will poison the relationships we hold dear. The solution lies in asking and allowing God to overwhelm us with His goodness, His grace, His love, His kindness and His care.

I want to encourage you: If you are overwhelmed right now, give it to God so that He can do something new in your heart and perspective.

That's what happened to me. I quit focusing on the bed, the hospital room and the surgeries, and I started looking at Jesus Christ—specifically through reading and meditating on His Word. As I allowed Him to overwhelm me with His very nature and character, I fell in love with Him all over again. At that point, it didn't matter that I was in the hospital because I believed that God was in control and that He had a plan for me—that He would bring about a good work through my difficulties.

The Word of God: When God Speaks, Listen!

Let's face it: We have selective hearing when it comes to God's Word. When the Lord speaks something to us that we find encouraging and pleasant, we are more than willing to listen. But when God speaks to us about the sin in our lives and calls us to take corrective action, we often resist. When God speaks to us about suffering, we want to plug our ears.

The reality is that it is vital to listen to what God is telling us—no matter what His subject matter may be—and accept it. Most of our problems really center on our unwillingness to listen to God's Word. How common is it for us to fight with the Lord and disagree with Him regarding His Word—and then wonder why we are experiencing conflict in our lives?

Some of our problems stem from a lack of consulting God's Word for counsel and wisdom *before* making a major decision. We carry out bad business decisions, bad economic decisions and bad relational decisions—all because we did not seek the instruction and direction of the Lord first. Then when those decisions go wrong, we are likely to get mad at the Lord! I implore each of us: If God is speaking, listen; if He is instructing, pay attention. And if God tells us no, don't forsake obedience. Submitting to God's Word and taking immediate action to do what He says are imperative.

God often communicates difficult words. How do we handle these? Let's take a cue from the prophet Jeremiah. Known as the "weeping" prophet, Jeremiah had a rough assignment from the Lord. We read that the Lord said to him:

Even if Moses and Samuel stood before Me, My mind would not be favorable toward this people. Cast them out of My sight, and let them go forth. And it shall be, if they say to you, "Where should we go?" then you shall tell them, "Thus says the Lord: 'Such as are for death, to death; and such as are for the sword, to the sword; and such as are for the famine, to the famine; and such as are for the captivity, to the captivity.' And I will appoint over them four forms of destruction," says the Lord: "the sword to slay, the dogs to drag, the birds of the heavens and the beasts of the earth to devour and destroy. I will hand them over to trouble, to all kingdoms of the earth, because of Manasseh the son of Hezekiah, king of Judah, for what he did in Jerusalem" (Jer. 15:1-4).

Let's imagine for a moment being Jeremiah—a man who is tender and sensitive and has a heart for people. God comes to him and says, in essence, "You know, Jeremiah, I have a ministry for you that no one else can do. I've had it with the Southern Kingdom. I'm upset with them and don't want to hear from them anymore. My judgment is coming down on Judah, and I will not relent. Now, I want you to tell the people that their end is near. I'm doing this because of the wickedness of King Manasseh, son of Hezekiah, for what he did to Jerusalem and to my prophet Isaiah." That is an unsettling assignment.

A brief word about Manasseh: He was, hands down, the most wicked king that Judah ever had on the throne. He sacrificed his own children in idol worship, he killed the prophet Isaiah by stringing him up between two trees and literally cutting him in half, and he wreaked havoc on the city of Jerusalem.

So, with the insight that Jeremiah was a sensitive and caring man, what can we surmise about how God's directive word to him made him feel? I'm sure he felt completely overwhelmed. (No doubt we would be, too!) The prophetic message that God asked Jeremiah to deliver to the people was one of suffering and death. How could he not be shaken?

The Word of God in Our Hearts

Sometimes we probably feel much the same way Jeremiah did upon being given such an unpleasant assignment. We might lament,

"God, why are You doing this? Why is my car breaking down? Why is my marriage a mess? Why are my kids rebelling?" Sometimes life becomes so overwhelming that we become paralyzed with inaction and lack of wisdom. But if the Word of God miraculously comes into a person's heart, it can transform his or her outlook. For example, Martin Luther happened to read, "The just shall live by faith" (Rom. 1:17), and that not only changed his heart and ministry, but also brought about the Reformation.

Truthfully, Jeremiah had been given a difficult, overwhelming task by God. But then the Word of God grabbed his heart and subsequently changed his perspective, as we read in Jeremiah 15:16: "Your words were found, and I ate them, and Your word was to me the joy and rejoicing of my heart; for I am called by Your name, O Lord God of hosts."

God's wrath against Judah had not changed. God's assignment for Jeremiah had not changed either. But Jeremiah realized that the Lord God had chosen him and that he was His child. He found joy in *God Himself*, in spite of the difficulty. God's Word can bring about the same perspective transformation for us. Let's examine four aspects of what God's Word can mean to us, even in the midst of trying and difficult circumstances.

The Word of God Is God's Personal Message

Let's look once again at Jeremiah 15:16. I can't count how many times I have heard people say, "Pastor Steve, I just wish God would speak to me personally." My answer is always the same: *"He has!* That is what the Bible is. It's God's personal message to you—the one whom He has created, chosen and loved." As His personal message to us, God's Word should be of utmost priority. Not only is it His personal message to us, but it's His love note, His instruction manual, His personal conversation and His autobiography as well. Still, we often overlook how critical it is to glean from the Word of

God on a daily basis. We get overwhelmed by our circumstances and beg God to speak to us, yet ironically our Bible sits on the coffee table without being opened.

Jeremiah "ate" up God's Word. He inhaled it, he consumed it, and he allowed it to take control of his life. The result was immense joy and rejoicing. Did Jeremiah's situation change? No. Did God's message to the people of Judah change? No. But Jeremiah's heart changed because he consumed God's Word and realized that God loved him and had chosen him to do this special, albeit discouraging and distressing, job.

Back to me in my hospital room: Like Jeremiah, I realized that it was possible for me to rejoice in *God Himself* despite my overwhelming circumstances. When I allowed God's Word to consume me—to overwhelm me—my perspective shifted, and I was able to see the circumstances I faced not as insurmountable problems, but rather as an opportunity for God to do a great work in my attitude, actions and character.

The understanding that God's Word is His personal message to us has great transformative potential. The Word of God shows believers what the Lord has done for us, how He is going to sustain and protect us and how He is going to ensure that each of us finishes the race and comes home to Him. The Word of God illuminated Jeremiah's mind and revolutionized the perspective of his heart.

The Word of God Is Our Joy

Do you believe it is possible to go through some really horrendous moments in your life and somehow still have joy? I do. But apart from God, it is impossible. No motivational speech, psychological counseling or other man-made effort will fill a person's heart with joy in the midst of trying circumstances. We need a word from God. Jeremiah discovered that God's Word was indeed his joy, stating, "Your word was to me the joy and rejoicing of my heart" (Jer. 15:16).

Notice how the psalmist likens the Word of God to something sweet in our mouth: "How sweet are Your words to my taste, sweeter than honey to my mouth!" (Ps. 119:103). The Word of God is sweet because of what it does. God's Word encourages us in the storm. It reminds us of His promise that even though this season might be difficult, it will pass. God's Word tells us how much we are loved and how much worth we have in His sight as His unique creation. God's Word reminds us of God's sovereignty over every event, and just as importantly, His Word promises eternal life. Is it any wonder that Jeremiah found joy in God's Word?

Someone might say to me, "Well, that's nice, Pastor Steve, but if you knew what I was going through, you would understand why I am not joyful."

Here is how I would respond: "Let me ask you something. Are you filled with bitterness? Are you consumed by hatred? Are you resistant to God working in your life? If so, I call you to repent. Let God restore you and feed you by His Word. Your situation may not change, but why be miserable? Wouldn't you rather have God's peace and joy in the midst of your trial than be upset and bitter?"

Bottom line, we need to get rid of the pride and submit to God. If I gave a man a choice between getting down on his knees in front of his wife and saying he was sorry or jumping out of an airplane at 30,000 feet with no parachute, which would he likely choose? He would probably go the way of the airplane because of pride! Does that seem ridiculous? Absolutely. In the same way, it's ridiculous to choose to stay upset and despondent in our trials instead of hearing a word from God that would change our hearts.

Jeremiah didn't resist God. Even though he was overwhelmed and discouraged, he sought out the Word of God and found joy in the midst of his trial. Let's follow his example.

The Word of God Is Our Sweet Meditation

The declarations of another psalm express the next aspect of God's Word for us to unpack. The psalmist exults, "May my meditation be sweet to Him; I will be glad in the Lord" (Ps. 104:34). In other words, our time with God in His Word should be a time of sweetness—a time for soaking up the Lord's presence and finding His Word to be sweet and savory to our soul. One of my favorite verses that captures the sweetness of meditating on God's Word is found in the Song of Solomon: "O my dove, in the clefts of the rock, in the secret places of the cliff, let me see your face, let me hear your voice; for your voice is sweet, and your face is lovely" (Song of Sol. 2:14). Truly the voice of the Lord is sweet.

The disciples experienced this truth as well. When they were hiding in the Upper Room out of fear after Jesus' crucifixion and resurrection, Jesus appeared and said, "Peace to you" (Luke 24:36). Some time earlier, when the disciples were in the midst of a bad storm, Jesus was sleeping; the disciples woke Him out of fear, and He spoke to the wind and waves: "Peace, be still" (Mark 4:39). Jesus' voice brought peace to the lives of His followers when He walked on earth. Similarly, for us, meditating on His Word—the way He speaks to us today—brings joy and sweetness.

The Word of God Is Our Delight

In spite of the difficulties we face in life, the Word of God can be a delight. The psalms are filled with declarations of this truth: for example, "I delight to do Your will, O my God . . ." (Ps. 40:8); "I will delight myself in Your statutes . . ." (Ps. 119:16); and "Your testimonies also are my delight . . ." (Ps. 119:24).

Most of us know personally that it is difficult to find joy in the midst of trials. While in the hospital, I struggled with a bit of an attitude. Yes, I wanted out of that place and was overwhelmed by the whole experience, but then the Word of the Lord came to me and I was broken; I was humbled and realized God had a purpose for my trial. In that place, His Word became my delight. This made a huge difference in my outlook and my attitude. If you were to ask any of the nurses, they would say they saw a change in my demeanor. I started to cooperate much better, to smile, and to act more pleasantly. Had my situation changed? No. I was still in the hospital with all the needles stuck in me; I was still in pain. Through His Word, however, the Lord showed me His great love and mercy and encouraged my heart. God's Word had indeed been my delight.

The Finding of God's Word

There are a few more things we can learn from our dear prophet, Jeremiah. Let's revisit Jeremiah 15:16 one more time: "Your words were found, and I ate them, and Your word was to me the joy and rejoicing of my heart; for I am called by Your name, O Lord God of hosts." Several truths from this verse instruct and direct us.

First, Jeremiah looked to God's Word for an answer—and His words "were found." Do we do this? Do we look for answers in God's Word when we are overwhelmed? Furthermore, do we study it and meditate on it? Do we truly seek out God's voice, through His Word, in difficult situations? When we come to the end of ourselves and pursue the Lord, it's then that He is most likely to do a major work in our lives. In fact, sometimes that is exactly what God is waiting for: for us to come to the end of our rope, so that we surrender completely to Him and allow Him to take absolute control.

Far too often, we try to fix things ourselves and keep control over our problems, which just makes them worse. When we reach a point at which we realize that we don't have the strength, the answers or the ability to fix the problems, this marks the beginning of our getting out of the way so that God can take over.

I'm not saying we should give up hope and quit. Rather, I'm talking about relinquishing control of the situation and all aspects of our lives to the Lord—turning over the reins to Him instead of trying to fix the broken parts ourselves. Giving up is not an option, because we have a God who can do the impossible. We have a God who can change our hearts and the hearts of those we care about. We have a God who loves us and died for us. He's not going to leave us dangling over the edge of a cliff. God will either change us or our situations, but either way, He will indeed work in and through us to bring about His good plan.

I remember an incident that took place about 20 years ago, through which God did a transformative work in my heart. I was really into playing racquetball at the time; in fact, I was pretty good and was definitely competitive. In this season, my wife had expressed to me that I was not home very much, and that it would be nice if she and I could spend some time together.

Normally, I played racquetball with other believers, but I had been challenged by some nonbelievers, so I went out that night to play. I can still picture the scene vividly. My partner and I were beating these guys, and I was reveling in it, when all of a sudden, I missed a shot and got so mad that I slammed my racket on the ground. Now here I was, the pastor of a large church, teaching people about the love and character of God, and I slammed my racket on the ground in front of these nonbelievers in a little tantrum.

When it was my turn to serve the ball, it only went about one foot in front of me before hitting the ground. I got even madder. Finally, realization dawned, and I looked down at my racket, which was broken in eight places.

My partner laughed, but the unbelievers questioned me: "Aren't you a Christian?"

I responded, "Yes, I am."

They continued to press: "And I thought that you went to Calvary Chapel South Bay? In fact, aren't you the senior pastor?"

In complete embarrassment and humiliation, I answered, "Yes, I am."

Then they asked, "Why are you so mad?"

I simply replied, "I have to go."

Driving home, I realized that my wife must have been praying. When I walked in the house, she asked, "How was your game?" I showed her the racket, and she said, "Good. Did God speak to you?"

I answered, "He did," and then asked her, "Were you praying?"

She said, "I was praying that God would help me speak to you." God certainly gave her an open door through His advance work on my heart. He can speak to a heart, and He definitely can change a heart.

Finding God's Word is just as vital for us as it was for Jeremiah. As we do so, we will begin to think differently—and then act differently. Taking God at His word changes our attitude toward the situations we encounter. The more we dive into God's Word, the more our actions change; and as we are transformed, people really take notice.

Eating Up God's Word

Second, once Jeremiah found God's Word, he ate it up! He didn't just sample it; he devoured God's Word. How many of us "taste" God's Word but leave it at that? Tasting, I think, looks like opening up our Bible, scanning a paragraph, and then closing it and going about our day's business. Perhaps we dabble in the Word or play with it, but we don't commit to it.

I've noticed over the years this same lack of commitment—this "tasting" instead of devouring—in the way some guys behave with girls they are dating. A young man might just string a girl along with words of playful fun. Or he might give her a "promise ring" instead of a full engagement ring and a proposal of marriage. Basically, the guy is saying, "Hey, I *may* want to marry you. I don't want you to move on or to go out with anyone else, but I am going to look around for the next six months and just make sure you're the one I really want." Really? How about a true commitment? How about just making a choice to marry her? Ladies, take note: If the guy strings you along or doesn't give you an engagement ring, my advice is to seriously think about moving on.

Similarly, we shouldn't just "taste" God—testing Him out to ascertain if we like what He has to say without making any commitment to Him and His Word. Jeremiah ate up God's Word. He was committed to the Lord and to the words of God, no matter how difficult his calling as a prophet might have been. Christians must learn to commit—to say in their hearts that there is no turning back from this walk with God. It sounds like this: "God, I'm in this with You all the way to the very end." When we eat up God's Word, we will be inspired and challenged to make this type of radical commitment to Him.

Rejoicing over God's Word

Finally, after we make that commitment to God's Word and "eat it," we will find that our hearts overflow with joy. Psalm 119:162 says, "I rejoice at Your word as one who finds great treasure." Indeed, the Word of God brings refreshment and rejoicing. That's exactly what happened to me in the hospital. Yes, I was overwhelmed. But then God spoke His Word to me, and it completely changed my perspective and my attitude. Nothing can cheer us up and bring rejoicing like God's Word ministering to our hearts. There is a difference between joy and happiness. Happiness comes to us through temporal things and lasts only momentarily. Joy is a deep and abiding frame of mind—an eternal perspective that flourishes even in the midst of suffering, trials and hardships. That's why we rejoice over God's Word: It brings lasting healing to our lives.

The Evidence of God's Word at Work

Jeremiah 15:17 says, "I did not sit in the assembly of the mockers, nor did I rejoice; I sat alone because of Your hand, for You have filled me with indignation." In other words, Jeremiah was saying, "I did not get involved with those who don't believe in You; I did not walk in their counsel; I did not even sit and listen to their garbage. Instead, I sat alone." Are we willing to sit alone?

Let me pitch out some hard questions for you to consider: As Friday night comes around, are you willing to stay home alone instead of going out to party and get drunk with friends who don't know Christ? Or say that cute guy at work calls you and asks you out to dinner. Are you willing to stay home alone and honor God instead of going out with an unbeliever?

Jeremiah was willing to stand alone on the Word of God instead of going along with the crowd who ignored the Lord. Are we willing to do the same?

Perhaps this statement describes you: "I'm overwhelmed; I can't handle life right now."

I would ask you, "Okay, are you willing to look to God? Are you willing to acknowledge His lordship in your life?"

If your answer is, "I am," then find God's Word, truly commit to diving in and devouring His Word—and your heart will be changed. That overwhelming situation will be colored in a different light. God's perspective will bring clarity and wisdom. And you will find joy and sweetness in the midst of your circumstances because God's Word has spoken to you and there is no going back.

STUDY QUESTIONS

1. Why do we need to listen to God when He speaks?
2. How can the Word of God give us joy in our difficult situations?
3. When we are overwhelmed with life's problems, why is it important to look to God's Word?
4. What does it mean to "eat up" God's Word?

∽ PRAYER ∽

Lord, forgive me for my lack of commitment to Your Word. I don't want to just "taste" any longer; I want to commit. I surrender to Your ways. I want to be consumed by Your words, and I yearn for Your law to be my delight. Overwhelm me with Your Word. I need all of Your Scriptures—not just the words that encourage me, but the words that convict and move me as well. I want all that You have for me, including Your full counsel within my life. Do Your mighty work within my heart—through Your Word—so that You can do a mighty work through my life, I pray. Amen.

10

Overwhelmed by God's Provision . . .

instead of what we don't have

To make ends meet, put the Lord between them.
T. J. BACH

*Look at the birds of the air, for they neither sow nor reap nor gather
into barns; yet your heavenly Father feeds them.
Are you not of more value than they?*
MATTHEW 6:26

Unemployment. Underemployment.
Foreclosure. Bankruptcy.

When we hear these words, one thing likely comes to mind: money struggles. It's true that we live in very difficult economic times. These dreaded words, instead of being headline-worthy, have become so common that we just shake our heads when we hear of another person who is facing one or more of these predicaments.

The subject of God's provision usually leads us to think in terms of financial resources. But His provision entails far more than economic needs. It can also cover concerns such as barrenness, singleness, persecution and mistreatment. Incidentally, it is helpful

155

to remember that God's provision is in fact centered on our "needs" more often than our "wants." Now, that doesn't mean that God never gives us "extras." Of course He does; He is a generous God. But He is primarily concerned with our deep needs; so oftentimes, the lessons and the character building that the Lord aims to produce through His provision for us extend far past our economic woes.

My dear reader, are you overwhelmed by economic stress? Or perhaps you are overwhelmed because of some other perceived need in your life. In this chapter, we will examine the story of Joseph, one of the sons of Jacob, from the book of Genesis. Joseph went through some of the most severe trials that anyone could ever experience, but he ended up as second-in-command of the kingdom of Egypt.

The reason I want to focus on the biblical story of Joseph is that no matter what hardships this godly man experienced, he always chose to see God's provision in the trial—trusting that God's hand was on him through each step of the journey. Joseph believed in the providence and sovereignty of God, and he was convinced that the Lord was weaving the purposes of His will into the story of his life. He did not question what God did (or didn't do). He was not bitter and did not hold any resentment. No matter where he found himself, Joseph served wholeheartedly. His hardships did not jeopardize his identity in the Lord. Wherever Joseph found himself, the hand of God was upon him. Therefore, many others were blessed by his leadership and wisdom. Even so, God taught Joseph quite a few lessons, and some of them were pretty rough. Let's look at these lessons together.

Joseph: Prospering as a Slave

What? Joseph, a slave? Genesis 39:1 explains, "Now Joseph had been taken down to Egypt. And Potiphar, an officer of Pharaoh, captain of the guard, an Egyptian, bought him from the Ishmaelites who had taken him down there."

Some background is necessary to understand the reason Joseph was taken down to Egypt. To a certain extent, we need to blame Jacob, Joseph's father, for the tragic events that took place in the lives of Joseph and his brothers. Jacob fostered an environment of jealousy and sibling rivalry among his sons by esteeming Joseph and Benjamin above his other boys. It's a sad situation when parents show favoritism toward certain children over the others. There's no doubt that it creates an atmosphere of resentment and anger among siblings, and understandably so. Over the years, the resentment built among Joseph's brothers, and the final blow came when Jacob gave Joseph a beautiful coat of many colors. When the brothers saw how their father elevated Joseph over them, they were furious and decided upon revenge. They threw Joseph into a pit with the intent of killing him. But Reuben, the firstborn of all the sons, encouraged his brothers not to kill Joseph because he didn't want his blood on their hands. So instead, when they noticed a caravan of traders coming their way, they quickly decided to sell Joseph for 20 shekels of silver (see Gen. 37:3-28).

So here we have a teenage boy—who is timid, who grew up inside his father's house, who was loved by his mother and estranged from his brothers—suddenly shackled and taken to Egypt to be sold as a slave. Upon arrival, Joseph was bought for the house of Potiphar, an Egyptian high official. What if we were to put ourselves in Joseph's shoes? This young man, who had been treated tenderly by his mother and favored by his father, was now in a foreign home in a foreign land, with nothing to his name. He had lost everything and had been unfairly treated and betrayed by the very people who should have loved and protected him—his own siblings. For multiple reasons, Joseph was in a painful and disheartening situation.

How did he react? Was he bitter and angry? Did he whine and complain? No, Joseph was a young man who loved the Lord and believed that God was with him no matter his circumstances. He didn't quit or give up. Instead, he chose to make the best of his situation and serve where, seemingly, God had placed him.

If we were all like Joseph—believing that nothing could touch us without going through God's hands first, and that no matter how bad things got, God had sovereignly allowed them to happen—then we would be forgiving, godly people who were able to persevere through our difficult circumstances. That is exactly what God wants. He doesn't want us to be overwhelmed by the hard situations in our lives, but to see His hand of provision on us in the midst of them. He wants us to be forgiving and not bitter, serving and not quitting. He wants us to make the best of whatever particular situation He has placed us in at this time. And He wants us to be people who build up and encourage instead of murmuring and complaining.

I love the verse that follows the announcement of Joseph's being sold to Potiphar: "The Lord was with Joseph, and he was a successful man; and he was in the house of his master the Egyptian" (Gen. 39:2). The Lord was with Joseph. What a simple yet incredible statement! No matter how dire Joseph's circumstances appeared, the Lord God was with him every step of the way. This verse speaks directly to us in our time as well. The Lord is with us.

Are you having problems at work? The Lord is with you at work. Are you having problems at home? The Lord is with you at home. Anywhere you go, the Lord is there, right beside you.

Whatever difficult and trying situations we face, the Lord is with us—and when the Lord is with us, we can rest assured that He is in control. He knows exactly what each of His children is going through, and He knows exactly what we need in terms of His provision from deep storehouses of grace and strength. Instead of being overwhelmed and afraid, we must trust the One who loves us and holds us in the palm of His hand. That's what Joseph did, and his rest and trust in God's sovereignty and omnipresence were reflected in his attitude and in the way that he prospered in the midst of his suffering.

It would be normal to wonder why I'm affirming that Joseph prospered when he was a slave. After all, in a very short period of time, he went from living in his father's tent to serving as a slave to a man he didn't know in a country that had a bad reputation among his people. How can this be seen as "prospering"? We have to look at the bigger picture: God had a plan for Joseph's life, and that plan involved much more than just Joseph's immediate situation. Along the way, as He worked according to His larger purposes, the Lord walked with Joseph and guided his steps through the provision of grace and strength. Because Joseph understood this principle, God was able not only to teach and transform him individually, but also to use him in a mighty way for the good of multitudes of people.

Let's continue to read about Joseph's journey: "The Lord was with Joseph, and he was a successful man; and he was in the house of his master the Egyptian. And his master saw that the Lord was with him and that the Lord made all he did to prosper in his hand" (Gen. 39:2-3).

So when Joseph's master, Potiphar, observed Joseph at work, he didn't see a young man standing in the corner doing nothing. He saw a boy pushing a broom, raking, wiping windows and otherwise keeping busy doing his job—because this was where God had put him. In a miraculous way, Joseph was able to understand that every place and every situation in which he found himself was exactly where God wanted him to be—and he was determined to make the best of it. He was not going to blame God, his parents, or even his brothers. Instead, his attitude was: "God, this is where You brought me, so help me to be the very best I can be."

What this young man couldn't even begin to fathom was that from the very beginning of time, God had ordained that he would save a nation from starvation. But before this plan of God would come to fruition, Joseph had to grow up and be molded into a mighty man of God. To accomplish this molding, God was going to lead Joseph on a very difficult road from the pit to the palace.

Joseph was going to have to pass some tests the Lord would bring his way—the test of being rejected by his family, the test of temptation to commit adultery, the test of being wrongly accused of a crime and thrown into prison and, finally, the test of forgiveness. In all of these situations, Joseph would rise above the difficult, unfair circumstances and tests he faced. How could he do that? The Lord brought His provision to Joseph in the form of His presence, and that's all he needed to succeed.

Serving God Without Question

Scripture records that Joseph was a faithful, steadfast servant to Potiphar: "So Joseph found favor in his sight, and served him. Then he made him overseer of his house, and all that he had he put under his authority" (Gen. 39:4).

Notice, it didn't matter that Joseph was in a foreign country (one that was not of a good reputation), working for a foreign dictator. What mattered was that Joseph was committed to doing the best job he could because he wanted to be faithful to God. In the same way, as believers, we should serve God with everything we have, right where He has placed us, without question. It doesn't matter if we're serving someone who is a believer or an unbeliever. What does matter is that we are reflecting the character and love of Jesus Christ. We are His representatives, so people will watch to see how we behave. Potiphar was impressed with Joseph and grasped who the Hebrew God was by the behavior of his slave.

When we understand the truth that God sovereignly orchestrates our lives, we will serve Him wholeheartedly, no matter where we are or what we are experiencing, without question. A terrible situation at home means we need to serve. Struggles with the kids indicate that service is necessary. Challenging circumstances and difficult problems should not alter who we are as believers in Christ. They should not make us so depressed that we cannot be the men and women God has called us to be.

Yes, your husband might be acting unkindly and not treating you right. Yes, your wife might be going through a time of depression and self-centeredness in her life. Yes, your boss may be horribly demanding and critical. Yes, the checkbook may be empty. And yes, your kids may be driving you to frustration, but no matter what your circumstances may be, you are still called to serve those whom God has placed in your life.

In actuality, it's not about serving your spouse, boss, friends, family or children anyway. It's about serving God and being faithful to Him, as the apostle Paul makes clear: "And whatever you do, do it heartily, as to the Lord and not to men, knowing that from the Lord you will receive the reward of the inheritance; for you serve the Lord Christ" (Col. 3:23-24). Because we are serving the Lord, not men, we can love, forgive and prosper right where we are, no matter how hard the trial might be.

God Blesses Others
Through Our Faithfulness

Joseph's story continues:

> So it was, from the time that he had made him overseer
> of his house and all that he had, that the Lord blessed the
> Egyptian's house for Joseph's sake; and the blessing of the

Lord was on all that he had in the house and in the field. Thus he left all that he had in Joseph's hand, and he did not know what he had except for the bread which he ate (Gen. 39:5-6).

As Joseph served faithfully, God poured out blessing, not only on Joseph himself, but also on Potiphar and everyone in his household and everything in his field. God increased Potiphar's livestock, crops, fruit trees and fields. Ultimately, Potiphar didn't even know how much he had anymore, concerning himself only with the food he ate, because he made Joseph the manager and overseer of everything in his household.

Here's a teenager who had lost his home, his family, and everything he possessed. Now, as a slave, this young man made his master a very wealthy man because his eyes were on God. He served, had a right attitude, and gave God his very best. As a result, not only did he prosper, but his boss also prospered.

If only this same attitude were engraved into the pathways of our lives! Can we believe with certainty that the Lord is with us right now at work? Is He with us in that relationship we're struggling with or in the midst of a tragedy or crisis? The answer is absolutely yes. God will never leave us or forsake us. In other words, He is watching over us and giving us His provision, and He has a calling on each of our lives.

In fact, He has predestined us (see Rom. 8:29). There's a reason why each of us was born. There's a reason why we're alive in this age, at this moment, and in this situation. God wants to use us in that hard place we find ourselves in right now. When we trust in God, He can save our family, our city or our business. In other words, God can do extraordinary things through us. But that will require that we stop resisting Him and trying to avoid the struggles. Instead of being overwhelmed—instead of being discouraged and wanting to quit—let's serve God wholeheartedly and trust Him both for His provision of grace and to work out His good in our lives.

God Is in the Good and the Bad

Joseph had to be prepared for becoming the ruler of a world power. He was a timid boy in many ways, but he was also proud. So the Lord had to mold and shape Joseph's character in order to make him a humble leader. How does God do something like that? In Joseph's life, He worked through a myriad of trials and experiences. Joseph was thrown into a pit. He was sold as a slave and then, sometime later, thrown into jail (even though he was innocent of the charges). Everywhere Joseph was placed, he served faithfully and developed the skills to become an expert administrator.

Too often, we don't see opportunities in our problems. We just see the problems, and we complain, "Why are You doing this to me, God? Why am I in this prison? Why am I in this pit? What's the purpose of this? I don't see what this is proving." God wants us to say instead, "I see You, God, and I want to give You thanks for the work You are doing in me. I am going to continue to serve right where You have put me." Remember Paul and Silas in the book of Acts? These faithful men were beaten and put in prison, but while there they didn't complain or get angry at God. Rather, they prayed and worshiped God, and then the Lord shook the prison doors open (see Acts 16:25-26). Notice that it's God who opens that prison door. He's the One who brings us out of the pit and prepares us to serve.

When he was in prison, Joseph didn't complain or assert that his situation wasn't fair. When he was a servant in Potiphar's house, he didn't ask when his slavery was going to be over. Rather, wherever he was placed, he served wholeheartedly and with complete dedication. Joseph trusted God throughout all of his trials, believing that the Lord had a plan for his life and would make provision in it.

In the same way, God also has a calling upon our lives—a supernaturally designed plan for each of us. That difficult place we currently find ourselves in may just be the training ground that God is using to make us a better parent, a better spouse, a better worker, a better steward and a better Christian. Our attitude should humbly be: "God, let me blossom where You have put me."

It's an absolute given that there will be bad times to suffer through. It's also likely—normal, even—that our human emotions will cause us to be overwhelmed by our problems. However, sometimes just when we think we have it as bad as we possibly could, the Lord opens our eyes to someone else's pain and suffering.

This happened to me when I was in the hospital getting some blood work done. A man who had just gone through a round of chemotherapy sat next to me. All morning, I had been whining and complaining about my troubles; then the Lord pierced my heart: "Stephen, look at this man and what he is experiencing right now." I took my eyes off of myself and my problems, and I began to pray with and minister to this man, as the Lord filled me with great compassion for him.

We may be legitimately overwhelmed by our problems, but there are others around us who are suffering, even dying, who could use our compassion, our touch and our concern. Recently, my wife and I had the privilege of having dinner and fellowship with the wife of Pastor Saeed, who is jailed in Iran for his sharing of the gospel with fellow Iranians. As we sat and listened to his wife, Naghmeh, share about her trust in the Lord, we were struck deeply by this woman's rock-solid faith. She was determined to follow God's will, even if that meant her husband would never be freed.

It's been a long time since I've seen this kind of commitment to Christ; Naghmeh's faith humbled me and convicted my heart. In my spirit, I was weeping and asking God to change me and help me to accept the trials in my life with greater faith and joy. When we see our problems in light of someone else's, it's amazing how diminished they become in our eyes as our perspective shifts. There are families all around us who are lost, but we are too busy to minister to them. Marriages need attention, but our hearts and minds are immersed elsewhere. Our kids are having a hard time, but we are too overwhelmed by our work to talk and pray with them.

It's often at these times that the Lord somehow gets our attention; when He does, our response should be, "God, what do You want?"

As we seek His will, He gently leads and corrects, with words that might sound like this: "My child, I want you to see Me in the good and in the bad. I want you to understand that nothing is going to come into your life or your heart unless I allow it. And if it does come to you, then it is what you need; it's My provision for you for your growth."

When God allowed the shackles to be put on Joseph in that prison, it was for good reason. I'm not talking about the obvious function of restraining Joseph's legs, although that's the superficial purpose a human eye would discern. I'm referring to the greater, supernatural purpose God had; He wanted the iron to go through the shackles into Joseph's heart, soul and spirit. God used those shackles and that prison cell to make Joseph into a man who would stand before a nation and lead with strength and compassion—and without fear.

Let's face it, sometimes Christians are weak and need to be taught fortitude and endurance. The smallest problem comes into our lives and we fall apart. Over the past 2,000 years, men and women of faith have endured great trials and persecution in bringing the gospel to people throughout the world. Some have been tortured; some have been separated from their families; and many have died cruel, unfair deaths because of their faith in Jesus Christ. In contrast, some Christians I know today get upset if someone looks at them the wrong way. We might get worked up if somebody doesn't say hi to us or if we feel ignored. Yes, we have some undeniable problems; I'm not belittling that fact. But in general, we Christians are much weaker than our forebears who experienced severe and desperate trials.

That being the case, we don't have a good handle on how to overcome the obstacles we face. This is a learned skill, but it begins with recognizing and believing that God is going to sustain us through our trials and make us more spiritual people with strength of character. It's a process of learning how to serve where we are planted and trust God with our future. Jesus reminded us that in this world we will have troubles (see John 16:33). Cars are going to break. Marriages are going to go through rough times. Children are going to try us and wear us out with their demands and immaturity. God has not rejected us; neither does He want us to quit, to lose our joy, or to become depressed. Just as Joseph did, we need to trust God—that He is in both the good and the bad—and serve in the midst of our trials.

When he experienced severe trials, Joseph was an innocent man. Through this, we see that sometimes horrible things happen to godly people. A car accident paralyzes our Christian friend. A child dies from a brain tumor. A Christian man loses his job, and his family goes bankrupt. A bomb goes off at a marathon in Boston and kills and maims innocent people. There is no understanding these tragedies.

Furthermore, when terrible things happen in our own lives, it just doesn't seem right or fair, does it? Even so, God is sovereignly in control. He allows trials for one purpose: to move us from the point where we are currently to the point where He wants us to be. He is growing us into people who are tender and compassionate, but have spirits of iron and steel—people whose faith is rock solid. When we've closed down the business, when we've struggled with an unwanted divorce or when we've gone through children running away or leaving the faith—when we've experienced trials of any magnitude—with some distance and reflection, we soon realize that God has redeemed our experience, and that we are stronger than we have ever been in our walk with the Lord. No one can take' that away.

Living with Victory Rather Than as a Victim

From a human perspective, Joseph was a victim of unfair treatment at the hands of others. His brothers threw him into a pit and then sold him as a slave; Potiphar's wife falsely accused Joseph of rape, which landed him in prison (see Gen. 39:7-20). In addition, when Joseph befriended and helped two fellow prisoners, the one who was released forgot all about him, even though he had promised to remember Joseph and show kindness to him (see Gen. 40).

There is no question that there are victims in our society today. Just turning on the news for an hour reminds us of that sordid fact. Humanly speaking, we have all been victims of someone else's mistreatment or unfairness at some point in this journey of life. But we can only use that excuse for so long. Continuing to live with a victim mentality will destroy us and those around us. It is essential that we experience a shift in which we begin looking at trials and tragedies from God's perspective and not that of a victim.

This is a sensitive and personal subject for me, because I was a victim of molestation when I was a young teenager. I was taken advantage of by someone I trusted—a teacher at school. It was the darkest time of my life. Quite a while later, however, I realized that although God certainly didn't cause this painful event, He had allowed it to happen. That sounds horrible to many, but when we accept that God is in control and that He uses everything in our lives, good and bad, it actually is a comfort to know that even this devastating incident was not beyond God's reach.

He has indeed used it for good—helping me to minister to those who have experienced the same pain. I don't view that period in my life as defining me. Rather, I have joy in my heart because I see God's hand upon me—and this is the attitude that is needed in order to achieve victory. We have to rise above our tragedy and live with victory in our hearts, which is something that God gladly gives provision for when we ask.

God Is with Us

Let's end our study of Joseph with the reminder that God is always with us and always at work in us. From a human perspective, it's logical to feel alone. However, it's a walk of faith to believe what is contrary to our feelings. Let's go back to Joseph in the pit:

> But Reuben heard it, and he delivered him out of their hands, and said, "Let us not kill him." And Reuben said to them, "Shed no blood, but cast him into this pit which is in the wilderness, and do not lay a hand on him"—that he might deliver him out of their hands, and bring him back to his father.
>
> So it came to pass, when Joseph had come to his brothers, that they stripped Joseph of his tunic, the tunic of many colors that was on him. Then they took him and cast him into a pit (Gen. 37:21-24).

Reading this account of Joseph's brothers' betrayal, we can't help but feel compassion for Joseph. After all, he had no idea what his brothers were going to do to him. All of a sudden, he was thrown into a horrible, empty pit—rejected by his own family.

Perhaps you can relate to Joseph. The problem you are facing right now—the one that has you overwhelmed—has it left you feeling barren and empty? Maybe you are thinking, *I don't feel God's presence.*

I don't know what's going on in my life, and I feel rejected by everyone I know. Truly, God must hate me. But think again. Although those are common human emotional responses to suffering, could it be that God has put you in this place so that you would look to the Lord alone for your sustenance and provision? Maybe the Lord wishes to show you that He's bigger than your family; bigger than your rejecting friends; and bigger than the pit, the barrenness and the loneliness that surround you.

When we look at the Bible, it is interesting to note that many women who were barren for a season ended up bringing forth children who served God. Men like Samson, Isaac, Jacob, Samuel and John the Baptist came forth from previously barren women. God made provision for these women; through the work of the Holy Spirit, He turned their barrenness into fruit. Similarly, God can take us out of the pit and bring forth fruit in our lives. Through His abundant life and provision, He removes barrenness and produces His fullness and joy.

Is it worth going through all these trials and tribulations? Yes it is, even though it may not feel that way when we are in the midst of our problems. When God begins to work in our lives, we are changed, and that results in blessing. Like a potter who shapes a bowl, God applies His perfect and omniscient hand of provision. He spins the wheel faster and faster; we ask, "What are You doing, God?" We start to get dizzy and begin to worry. God stirs the water and begins to shape us.

When His fingers produce the difficult circumstances that will mold our character, we often protest because the process causes us pain. His finger may take away the boyfriend or girlfriend who is causing us to sin. Another finger may eliminate our job. Yet another finger may take away our health. A typical reaction to this pain and suffering is to scream and complain and get angry at the Potter. The Potter responds, "There's no reason to be angry with

Me. The clay doesn't tell the Potter what to do. I know what I am doing. I'm molding you into the person I want you to be. I am at the wheel, and I am controlling the speed. Trust Me."

As God's creative work in our lives continues, the oven and its 750-degree heat produce more sweating and struggling. Perhaps we say to God, "What is this all about?" But God is with us in that oven. He walks hand in hand with us as the heat blasts. As the trials and tribulations do their work of molding us into the people He wants us to be, He never leaves our side. Do you recall the story of Shadrach, Meshach and Abed-Nego in the fiery furnace? These three faithful young men were not alone in the heat. The Lord was right there with them, protecting them each step of the way (see Dan. 3:19-25).

When the pottery comes out of the oven, it looks majestic. It's glossy and beautiful. The imperfections have been worked out, and the piece has been made whole. God knows what He's doing. He will never leave us nor forsake us. In every moment of our lives, even in every crisis and trial, as "the Lord was with Joseph" (Gen. 39:2), we too can say with confidence, "The Lord is with me."

Faith is believing that no matter what our circumstances are, God will do a work deep in our hearts. Our job is to continue serving, loving, trusting His provision and being cheerful before God. No matter how tough it gets, He wants us to know that He has allowed this trial and this suffering to happen for a purpose. If we are in the pit, then God is going to use it to get us to Egypt. If we are in Potiphar's house as a slave, then God wants us to serve well so He can raise us up. If we are thrown in prison, even unjustly, then God is going to use us there as well.

Our attitude and outlook are of great importance. We cannot gripe, complain, murmur or quit. If there's ever a time that we must draw deep on faith—"the evidence of things not seen" (Heb. 11:1)— and believe that God is totally sovereign and always at work, it's right now. We must trust and be overwhelmed by God's provision of the trial with the underlying purpose of bringing about amazing growth in our maturity and faith. God is doing a major work of His supernatural and miraculous provision through this trial, and ultimately, we are going to shine. We will bring hope to those around us, and others will be blessed through our faithfulness to God.

STUDY QUESTIONS

1. When we are facing difficult situations, what does God want us to know?
2. Why does God bless others through our faithfulness?
3. Why does God allow the good and the bad things to happen in our lives?
4. Why must we stop living our lives with a victim mentality?

∾ PRAYER ∾

Thank You, Lord, that Your hand is always upon my life and that You never leave me alone. Thank You that I am the apple of Your eye and that Your plans for me are always good. Help me to remember these things when I am in the dark places along the road of life and when I cannot seem to see the dawn. Overwhelm me with Your provision, I pray. Remind me that You are good, and never let me forget Your promises. I know Your Holy Spirit will lead and guide me; help me to stand firm and remember in faith that wherever I am is right where You have allowed me to be. Thank You that I am never out of Your reach. Amen.

11

Overwhelmed by God's Victory . . .

instead of spiritual defeat

The devil found defeat in victory at the cross;
the Christian finds victory in defeat at the cross!
ANONYMOUS

Therefore submit to God. Resist the devil and he will flee from you.
Draw near to God and He will draw near to you. Cleanse your hands,
you sinners; and purify your hearts, you double-minded.
JAMES 4:7-8

Do you ever feel like a war is taking place inside you? Perhaps you want to do what is right before the Lord, but you find yourself doing the exact opposite.

I heard a great little story that I want to share with you because it clearly shows the warfare that we engage in on a daily basis:

There was a couple who had been fighting for weeks over the purchase of a new car. The husband wanted a sports car so that he could zip through traffic, in and out of town—so that he could get to church more quickly, of course. The wife, on the other hand, wanted a new kitchen stove so that she could cook better. The discussion was getting very heated.

Finally the husband shouted, "Look, I want something that goes from 0 to 300 in four seconds or less. And that's all there is to it." When the wife started to present and prove her point, the husband shut her out of his mind, becoming angrier and angrier, and thinking about how his needs were always pushed to the bottom of the list. He couldn't understand why his wife did not see how his need for a new car with a nice speaker system far outweighed her desire for a new, nicer kitchen stove.

All of a sudden, the husband was brought back to reality when he heard his wife say, "Have you heard anything I said?"

The husband replied, "I work hard and I deserve it." Then he added, "My birthday's coming up next week. You'd better surprise me or I'm going to have a fit!"

When the big day came, he woke up early and dashed out to the garage, but there was no new car. Feeling angry, he went back into the house, looking for his wife, but she was not home—a wise woman. Flustered and upset, he went into the bathroom to get ready for the day. Lo and behold, sitting on the floor, wrapped in a red ribbon, was a brand-new scale with a note that said, "Honey, this will go from 0 to 270 in two seconds. Happy Birthday!"

As Christians, we are in a battle every day of our lives. Some believers see this earthly existence only as a playground, but the reality is that our soul is a battlefield—one on which Satan and God are both seeking to triumph! Each person is divided into three areas: the spirit, the soul and the flesh. These three aspects of our selves were never meant to be looked at as three different or distinct areas, as often is the custom in our modern world. Instead, they should be looked at as three interrelated components functioning as one entity. So when our spirit is weak, it affects our flesh and our soul. The spirit, soul and flesh, though three separate parts of our being, are intricately connected to one another.

When God made Adam and Eve and put them in the Garden of Eden, He made them spirit, soul and flesh. They had perfect fellowship with God because their spirit was the dominant aspect of their being. God's Spirit connected with their spirit, and they had instant and unbridled fellowship. However, God told Adam that the day he ate of the forbidden tree, he would die. Adam and Eve did eat from that tree, and their eyes were suddenly opened to their flesh—and they were ashamed. They tried to cover their flesh—to hide it, so to speak—but God saw their attempt to hide their sin, and it did not meet His righteous requirements. Therefore, God killed an animal, took its skin, and covered Adam and Eve with the blood sacrifice (see Gen. 2-3).

When Adam and Eve sinned, their spirit diminished and their flesh took the lead—changing the divine order and separating mankind from fellowship with God. Thousands of years later, when Jesus Christ died on the cross and rose again, He became the bridge between humans and God. By believing on Him, we can once again be restored to fellowship with God. Our spirit can once again be in the lead! However, because we are the children of Adam, sin is a part of who we are, and our flesh is still contending for that lead role in our lives.

So we are in a battle—a war waged within; it's the battle between our flesh and our spirit. Not one of us escapes this battle. It's a part of the Christian life. But too many of us are overwhelmed and defeated, succumbing to the desires and the lusts of the flesh instead of yielding to and walking in the power of the Holy Spirit. We forget that we are not alone in this battle. The apostle Peter, who constantly had difficulty battling with the flesh, wrote about this ongoing warfare: "Beloved, I beg you as sojourners and pilgrims, abstain from fleshly lusts which war against the soul" (1 Pet. 2:11).

The apostle Paul described the same struggle: "For the flesh lusts against the Spirit, and the Spirit against the flesh; and these are contrary to one another, so that you do not do the things that you wish" (Gal. 5:17). It's clear that there is a war being waged inside of us on a daily basis. We want to go out and live in the world, but the Spirit is convicting us. We want to make a real commitment to God, but the flesh tries to derail us. As Christians, we were given a new nature when we accepted Jesus Christ as our Lord and Savior. That new nature, which is of the Spirit, is vying for control over our fleshly sinful nature. In his letter to the Galatians, Paul went on to describe just how different the two natures are:

> Now the works of the flesh are evident, which are: adultery, fornication, uncleanness, lewdness, idolatry, sorcery, hatred, contentions, jealousies, outbursts of wrath, selfish ambitions, dissensions, heresies, envy, murders, drunkenness, revelries, and the like; of which I tell you beforehand, just as I also told you in time past, that those who practice such things will not inherit the kingdom of God.
>
> But the fruit of the Spirit is love, joy, peace, longsuffering, kindness, goodness, faithfulness, gentleness, self-control. Against such there is no law. And those who are Christ's have crucified the flesh with its passions and desires. If we live in the Spirit, let us also walk in the Spirit. Let us not become conceited, provoking one another, envying one another (Gal. 5:19-26).

The fruit of the Spirit is what we desire to see manifested in our lives, but so often the works of the flesh are instead displayed in our thoughts and actions. It's a battle that we fight on a daily basis—a war within us that needs to be won.

The War Within Us

In his epistle, James explains that the war within comes from the problem of lust:

> Where do wars and fights come from among you? Do they not come from your desires for pleasure that war in your members? You lust and do not have. You murder and covet and cannot obtain. You fight and war. Yet you do not have because you do not ask. You ask and do not receive, because you ask amiss, that you may spend it on your pleasures. Adulterers and adulteresses! Do you not know that friendship with the world is enmity with God? Whoever therefore wants to be a friend of the world makes himself an enemy of God. Or do you think that the Scripture says in vain, "The Spirit who dwells in us yearns jealously"? (Jas. 4:1-5).

Notice that this Scripture passage makes it clear that our inner war and conflicts come from our lusts. James mentions our lusts four times in this passage. Lust is a passion—a strong desire for things that are contrary to God's Word. When we lust after something, we are following our sinful desires instead of God's desire for our life. Instead of lusting after the things of the flesh, God desires that we would have passion for Him. I've heard it said, "What is lust? It's a natural, normal longing that oversteps the limits that God appoints."

The truth of this definition is easily seen when it comes to the issue of sex. Sex is a pleasure and gift that God ordained to be enjoyed in the context of a loving, committed, lifelong marriage. When we step outside of the boundaries that God has set, we lust instead of love, and that sets up numerous problems, perversions and immorality. How can we not see that in our world today? Pornography, pedophilia, rape, sexual addiction, homosexuality, "hooking up," fornication, adultery and other lusts have so permeated our society that it's common to begin seeing some of these things as "normal." But God's Word clearly defines the boundaries, and crossing over His line means we are being led by our lusts.

Satan works in conjunction with our fleshly desires to tempt us to overstep God's boundaries, while the Holy Spirit, who lives in us and has given us a new nature, prompts us to do what is right in God's eyes—to stay within the Lord's parameters for our lives. So, it's simple to see why we have a war going on inside us! The battle between our spirit and our flesh also involves our soul, which includes our mind, emotions and will. The Bible tells us that if we yield to the Spirit, we're going to be spiritually minded, which brings life and peace. If we yield to the flesh, we're going to be carnally minded, which leads to death (see Rom. 8:5-6). So, our soul is in the middle; the Spirit of the living God is seeking to control it, and the enemy of our soul, Satan, is also trying to grab it.

If we yield our members to unrighteousness, it means that we have surrendered, by our own choice, and given Satan the advantage. So now, these two—our flesh and our minds (as well as our emotions and our wills)—have joined camps, and we are going to feed the body's appetite. This leads to the living of a carnal life and therefore an emptiness concerning the Spirit of God.

If we choose to live under the authority of the Spirit, however, we are feeding our souls and transforming our minds. When we yield to the Spirit, we are living according to God's will, and our emotions are now the fruit of the Holy Spirit. It is through yielding to the Spirit that we can gain victory over the flesh. The apostle Paul said, in effect, "I reckon the old man dead" (see Rom. 6:11), and, "I buffet, I beat, I bring under subjection this body" (see 1 Cor. 9:27). The reason he used this kind of terminology is that the real us is not our flesh. Rather, the real us is our spirit, which is directed by the Spirit who lives inside of us.

It is our spirit that has been redeemed. Our flesh is not redeemed. It's not until we go to heaven that we will get a new body—one that is not corruptible. So, for now, as believers, our redeemed spirits live inside unredeemed bodies. That's why we experience this internal war. Every day of our lives, we each have to make a decision about whether we are going to yield to the Spirit or yield to our flesh.

I heard a short story once that offers helpful insight into this battle: A car dealership decided to do a gimmicky contest to get people to come to their lot. They took two of their trucks and backed them up to each other so that the tailgates were facing each other. They then tied a rope onto one of the bumpers and took the other end of the rope and tied it onto the other truck's bumper. Which truck would win the tug-of-war? Unbeknownst to the onlookers, one truck had gasoline in the tank and the other truck was empty. The winner, of course, would be the truck that had gasoline in its tank! In the same way, if we fill (feed) the flesh, it will win the tug-of-war, and the result will be a carnal mind. However, if we fill (feed) the Spirit, He will win the tug-of-war, and the result will be a victorious Christian walk.

Having established the fact of a constant battle between the Spirit and the flesh in the life of a believer, let's now look at the reason for the conflict, the result of the conflict and the reality of the conflict.

The Reason for the Conflict

Do we have conflicts in our lives? Do we have fights at home—with our spouse and kids? Do we have disagreements at work? Absolutely. There's a reason for all of these. The sooner we understand the battle taking place in the spiritual realm, the better off we're going to be. Too often, we are completely oblivious to the war that rages within us.

In the Garden of Gethsemane, Jesus battled His flesh. He didn't sin, but according to the Bible, He was tempted in all ways, just as we are (see Heb. 4:15). That night in the garden, Jesus agonized to the point of sweating drops of blood. He asked His disciples to stay awake and pray with Him, but they kept falling asleep. Jesus said, "Could you not watch with Me one hour?" (Matt. 26:40). If they had stayed awake, they would have witnessed the incredible victory Jesus achieved because He prayed His way through the conflict. There is no doubt that the Lord wanted them to understand the importance of praying through spiritual battles.

We have a much greater ability to understand this warfare than Jesus' original disciples did because we have the Word of God. From Scripture, we learn that our battles are not against flesh and blood, but against powers and principalities and the rulers of darkness (see Eph. 6:12). Satan is seeking to worm his way into every one of our relationships. Furthermore, he is seeking to turn us away from God and to have us go a different way than the way of the cross. The possibility exists that we can accept Christ as our Savior, but still not yield to the Spirit in our lives. We can live for God, but not go the way of the cross. We can begin to read our Bibles, but not pray. If Satan can't keep us from salvation, he will try to keep us from walking with the Lord and attempt to hinder us from being effective and victorious in our Christian lives.

Now, where does all this conflict originate? It comes from our flesh fighting (or rebelling) against the things of God. Before we are saved, there is enmity between us and God, which means that we are at war with God.

You might well think, *I've never been mad at God.* Your sin nature, however, is constantly fighting God and His laws and ways. Our sinful nature would never allow us to stand in the presence of God's glory. So, God sent Christ to stand in the gap—to be the bridge between humanity and God. Because of Jesus Christ and His

180

righteousness, we can now have fellowship with God. We have been born again, this time not of the flesh, but of the Spirit of God. Now we have the ability to live a godly life because the Lord has sent His own Spirit to reside in us. Even so, our old, sinful nature still resides in us as well, and these two factions are in a constant battle for control of our lives.

Does this tug-of-war sound familiar? "God, I want to go this way."

"Stephen, I want you to go that way."

And it's a war.

"Well, God, why can't I go this way?"

"Stephen, I told you I want you to go the other way."

Yielding to our flesh leads to feeling distant from God. Though we are not separated from God relationally (that is, He is still our Father), our sin does interfere with our fellowship with God. That's why it's important to confess our sin and repent of it, instead of hiding it, denying it or running from it. The more we try to hide from it, the greater our separation from God and the greater the likelihood we will continue yielding to our flesh.

Consider this example. Those of us who are parents will understand that we might get upset with our child and have to discipline him by sending him to his room. The relationship is not lost—that is, he is still our child—but the lines of communication (fellowship) have been temporarily closed. "I don't want to see you right now. Go to your room."

Now, how does the child get out of his room and back into your good graces? He knocks on your door and says, "Daddy (or Mommy), I'm sorry for what I did."

Repentance and forgiveness restore fellowship. God doesn't want to hear our excuses or our blaming of others for our sins. The Lord wants us to come clean—to confess, repent and seek His forgiveness!

Not only do we have a war going on inside of us, but we also have to deal with outward contentions—for example, someone cuts us off on the road; someone makes a hurtful comment; or someone ignores our calls and emails. So we get hurt, we feel pain or we get frustrated. All of these emotions then churn around in our minds and hearts, and we must make a choice about whether we will yield to the Spirit or to our flesh.

The truth is, too often we don't want to live the way God tells us to live. We would rather live a carnal life. So the war rages on, because God brings conviction to our hearts about the decisions we have made, the sin we have committed and the rebellion we have entertained. When we rebel against God's Word and yield to our fleshly nature, we quench (or grieve) the Holy Spirit and His work in our lives. We tend to treat the Holy Spirit like a "thing of power" instead of as a person—the third person of the Godhead. It is not possible to quench or grieve a thing. We can yell all we want at a chair, for example, but the chair is not going to feel sad or angry that we are yelling at it. We can only quench or grieve a person. Too often, we ignore the fact that the Holy Spirit is indeed a person—a part of the Trinity.

The Holy Spirit seeks to glorify Christ in our lives and is there to help us, teach us, chasten us, convict us and quicken us to Christ, who gave Himself for us. Because the Holy Spirit is there to help and encourage us to love and grow in the knowledge of Jesus Christ, it is baffling why we would ever want to hinder, grieve, quench or even resist Him. The reason for this strange behavior comes from our internal battle against the flesh.

So what does it mean to quench the Holy Spirit? Let's use an analogy: Imagine your wife has a great dinner waiting for you at home, but when you stop to buy gas for the car, you also pick up a couple of packs of Twinkies. On the drive home, you end up eating all the Twinkies. When it's time to sit down for dinner, you realize you are not hungry. You have quenched your hunger with the

Twinkies and have no desire to eat the wonderful meal in front of you!

Likewise, our spirit has a hunger for God, but when we choose to yield to our flesh, we end up quenching that hunger for God. When we resist the Holy Spirit, we quench the work He is doing in our lives. And every time we reject the counsel of God, we grieve the Holy Spirit and once again quench His work in our lives.

Think back for a moment: At any point in your life, has God or the Holy Spirit spoken to you and told you what to do, but you didn't do it? If so, you are not alone. The Bible recounts the stories of many people who resisted the counsel of God, often with dire consequences.

Adam and Eve were told not to eat from one particular tree in the Garden of Eden. There were many other trees from which Eve could have eaten, but the one that was off limits was the one that she desired. She saw it. She wanted it. She ate of it—thereby disobeying God (see Gen. 3:1-6). Achan was instructed not to take anything of the accursed items from Jericho. But he saw things he wanted and, against Joshua's orders, took them. Death was the result (see Josh. 7). King David, from the roof of his palace, saw Bathsheba bathing and wanted her; he took her and then tried to cover his sin. An innocent man, a child and a grandfather lost their lives because David yielded to the lust of the flesh (see 2 Sam. 11:1-12:19).

Bottom line, there is a war going on within each of us. Will we surrender to the flesh or to the Spirit?

The Result of the Conflict

The apostle James gets right to the point: "You lust and do not have. You murder and covet and cannot obtain. You fight and war. Yet you do not have because you do not ask. You ask and do not receive, because you ask amiss, that you may spend it on your pleasures" (Jas. 4:2-3).

We are lusting, which means our flesh is out of control. All we can think about is what we want. Because we don't have the things we want, we try to take them and end up hurting people. Our lust pushes us to step on people, deceive them, take from them and ignore their needs and feelings. So the war rages within us because we don't trust God. We resist His counsel and His Word regarding our lives, because we don't have faith that He will work things out according to what we truly need. If we trusted God with our desires—if we really believed that He knows best and will bring about in our lives His perfect and good will—then we would let go and stop trying to make things happen in our own ways and according to our own timing. God will give us all the things that we need. He will not hold anything back from us because He knows what's good for us.

In other words, we need to remember and believe God's sovereignty—His complete control over all circumstances in life. Instead of worrying about people squeezing us out of a job, or worrying about how we will meet that special person to marry, or worrying about how to pay the bills on such little income, we need to trust God and not yield to our lusts. When all is said and done, if God wants us to have a certain thing or desire, it's ours—no one on this earth can prevent that from happening. There is no need to "help" God out by taking matters into our own hands and giving in to our lusts. Too often, though, that's exactly what we do. Then, when we see the devastating results of our efforts, we ask God, "Why?"

Let's examine these verses from James 4 more closely. Verse 2a: "You lust and do not have." In other words, our lust does not bring us the pleasure that we sought. Our lust does not result in satisfaction. Verse 2b: "You murder and covet [lust] and cannot obtain." In other words, our passion is uncontrollable. We will not stop at anything in our attempts to fulfill our lust; we lose all perspective and throw away all boundaries in the pursuit of plea-sure. Remember how King David killed Uriah so he could have Bathsheba? As a result, God allowed David's baby to die. Ahab mur-dered Naboth because he wanted his vineyard, but ultimately Ahab lost it all (see 1 Kings 21:1-22).

Verse 2d: "You do not have because you do not ask." This is about untapped potential. We should be asking God about our heart's desires—He may want to give them to us. When we fail to ask Him for what we want, and instead take matters into our own hands, we are leaving God out of the picture and not realizing the potential we may be forfeiting. Verse 3: "You ask and do not receive, because you ask amiss, that you may spend it on your pleasures." Here, God is not answering our prayer because we're asking Him for something that will not benefit us—something that will actually be a hindrance in our spiritual walk. In other words, our prayer request has nothing to do with God's glory and bringing about His will; rather, it is about what we desire and lust after—our perceived need to make ourselves happy.

How about these prayers? "Oh, God, please give me a million dollars." (Can God trust you with a million dollars? What exactly do you plan to do with all that money?) "Lord, if You will just give me this car, I can get to church more quickly." "Lord, if You would just change my wife, I would really be happy." "Oh, Lord, bless me, comfort my heart, give me that hunky-dory feeling. No cross; give me the crown. No pain; give me a pleasant Christian walk. Help me to shine for the glory of God. Lord, bless me, bless me, bless me. Lord, help me, help me, help me." If we are not careful, God be-comes a Santa Claus or a buffet in our minds. We pick and choose what we want, because we lust after things that will bring us instant gratification, happiness, pleasure and comfort.

What is God's will for our lives? First Thessalonians 5:23 gives us a clue: "Now may the God of peace Himself sanctify you completely; and may your whole spirit, soul, and body be preserved blameless at the coming of our Lord Jesus Christ."

Ultimately, God wants us to be completely sanctified in our spirit, soul and body. As we consider what this verse means in terms of the day-to-day decisions we must make about our Christian walks, it's important that we look at the order in which the three aspects of the self are mentioned. Notice that the spirit is listed first and the body last. Now, let's be really honest for a moment. What do we pray for most often? Our body. "Lord, help me lose weight . . . look good . . . grow hair . . . drive a nice car . . . live in a nice house . . . and oh, yes, give me money." We are quite often more concerned about our flesh than our spiritual needs.

God, however, wants our spirit to be the priority in our lives. In other words, He wants us to seek Him with all of our hearts. The Bible tells us that if we "seek first the kingdom of God and His righteousness, [then] all these things shall be added to [us]" (Matt. 6:33). If we put God first in our lives, we will soon realize that our outlook has changed. We may go ahead and buy that new car, but we will do so without lusting for it. And when we put God first, we may realize that we don't need that bigger, fancier house after all.

As we put the Lord first in our lives, God will transform our minds by renewing our thoughts through His Word. He will plant His desires in our hearts to the point that we can say, "Not my will but Yours be done." Furthermore, as we put God first, we will discover that we are feeding our spirit more and our flesh less—and we will notice a major change in our lives. Our thoughts will start reflecting God's thoughts; our emotions will start manifesting the fruit of the Spirit; and our decisions and desires will start lining up according to God's Word instead of our flesh.

If we are walking with God and putting Him first in our lives, it is much more likely that we are going to make great decisions. We don't have to worry about the little stuff or be overwhelmed by our problems. We don't have to live in defeat; instead, we can live in God's victory. On the other hand, when we put ourselves first over God and feed the flesh, it is a given that we will live in warfare.

The Reality of the Conflict

Continuing our exploration of James 4, we read, "Adulterers and adulteresses! Do you not know that friendship with the world is enmity with God? Whoever therefore wants to be a friend of the world makes himself an enemy of God" (Jas. 4:4).

Our problem is not that we are in the world, but that we allow the world to get into us. Truthfully, sometimes it's hard to tell the difference between a believer and a nonbeliever by the way they live—and this should not be the case. We can't help but exist in the world and society in which we live. The above verse certainly takes that into consideration. Notice its distinction: It talks about the problem with being a "friend" of the world. What does that mean?

When we are a friend of the world—understanding "the world" to be the way our culture thinks, the things our culture values, and the issues that our culture exalts—then we are embracing our culture's values, ethics and beliefs rather than God's. Now, one of my readers might be thinking, *Pastor Steve, I believe God's Word, not the culture.* But I would urge all of us to engage in a little self-examination: Do we watch what the culture watches? Do we sing what the culture sings? Do we do what the culture does? Do we value what the culture values?

The world feeds our fleshly appetite. Our culture encourages sexual promiscuity and perversion, fosters greed and self-gratification, and exalts selfishness. Bottom line, our culture encourages our lust for all that is opposed to God. The closer we draw to the things of this world, the further we pull away from God. So, instead of fostering friendship with the world, we need to have a light touch with the things of this world. We must be able to move away from the values of our culture and cling to the values that God has ordained and established for our lives.

The apostle Mark addresses the dangers of letting the world's cares and values seep into our hearts: "The cares of this world, the deceitfulness of riches, and the desires for other things entering in choke the word, and it becomes unfruitful" (Mark 4:19). Here is the key to real happiness in the Spirit: learning how to live with a light touch upon this world.

Now let's consider James 4:5, which gives us a glimpse of what happens in the heavenlies when we seek after the world: "Or do you think that the Scripture says in vain, 'The Spirit who dwells in us yearns jealously'?" Let me offer a different translation: "The Spirit which He made to dwell in us jealously yearns for our entire de-votion." I like that. The implication is that when we seek after the things of this world, the Spirit becomes jealous and is going to come after us. For example, when we begin to date a nonbeliever, the Spirit of God is going to shake up our lives.

You might react with a complaint like, "Pastor Steve, that's not fair!" Actually, dear believer, it is fair. Let's consider a parallel ex-ample from our own parenting: If we are with our child at a park and see a pit bull coming straight toward our child, we are going to intervene. We are going to do what we have to do to protect our child from being hurt by that pit bull. Does that mean we hate pit bulls? No. But we are jealously guarding our child from harm. We are go-ing to take action to ensure that the pit bull does not kill our child! That's the way God operates with us. He jealously wants us and will not share us with anyone else. He will do what it takes to protect us from anything that will harm us.

When we walk away from God, He's jealous. Remember Jonah? When Jonah took off, God went after him. When Peter took off, God went after him, too. Similarly, when we take off, God comes after us. We are His children, and He will not let go of us.

Seven Steps to Freedom and Victory

Are you tired of feeling defeated? Are you tired of giving in to your flesh time and again? As we read further in James' epistle, we can mine seven very practical steps to freedom and victory:

> But He gives more grace. Therefore He says: "God resists the proud, but gives grace to the humble."
>
> Therefore *submit to God. Resist the devil* and he will flee from you. *Draw near to God* and He will draw near to you. *Cleanse your hands*, you sinners; and *purify your hearts*, you double-minded. Lament and *mourn* and weep! Let your laughter be turned to mourning and your joy to gloom. *Humble yourselves* in the sight of the Lord, and He will lift you up.
>
> Do not speak evil of one another, brethren. He who speaks evil of a brother and judges his brother, speaks evil of the law and judges the law. But if you judge the law, you are not a doer of the law but a judge. There is one Lawgiver, who is able to save and to destroy. Who are you to judge another?
>
> Come now, you who say, "Today or tomorrow we will go to such and such a city, spend a year there, buy and sell, and make a profit"; whereas you do not know what will happen tomorrow. For what is your life? It is even a vapor that appears for a little time and then vanishes away. Instead, you ought to say, "If the Lord wills, we shall live and do this or that." But now you boast in your arrogance. All such boasting is evil.
>
> Therefore, to him who knows to do good and does not do it, to him it is sin (Jas. 4:6-17, emphasis added).

Let's take a closer look at these seven steps to freedom.

Submit to God

The first critical step is to submit to God. If we're saying to ourselves, "I'm fighting the Holy Spirit . . . I'm going after carnal things . . . I know that I shouldn't be in this relationship . . . I'm not really trusting God," then it's necessary to submit to God. James assures us, "But He gives more grace. . . . God resists the proud, but gives grace to the humble. Therefore submit to God" (vv. 6-7). He gives more grace—I love that. We know that we have done wrong. We're depressed and overwhelmed. It's beautiful that He's not going to say, "I told you not to do that." Instead, He gives us more grace. Then, because He gives us this tremendous grace, we are to "submit to God." This starts us on the path toward victory over our fleshly desires.

Think about this: If you're flying an airplane and are not sure of your location, what do you do? When you are lost, the first rule of aviation is to climb to a higher altitude. Why? Because you can't be sure if there is a mountain in front of you, so you want to go as high as you can to stay out of danger. Second, you begin to communicate with the tower and the air-traffic controllers. You don't skirt the issue or argue with them; rather, you come clean and confess that you are lost. The air-traffic controllers then begin to guide you in the right direction; if you want to make it out of your predicament safely, you will listen carefully to their instructions.

Similarly, submitting to God means that we pray, "I'm lost. I'm confused. I'm in trouble. I've done my own thing, and now I'm burned out. I'm overwhelmed. I'm ready to come back and submit to what You said. You are right, Lord; I'm wrong." God gladly responds to that kind of prayer. What do we submit to Him at this critical juncture? We submit our minds, our wills, our hearts and our bodies.

When the angel Gabriel visited Mary to tell her the glorious news that she would be the human instrument to bring the Savior into the world, she willingly submitted her body to God. But we often hold back our flesh when we submit to God, don't we? We think, *Oh, I'll give God my mind, my heart and my soul, but my body is mine.* Well, our body is a hunk of dirt. Why do we want to hold on to it? We may be in the mess we are in right now because we simply won't submit everything to God. Submission to God means we quit doing things our own way. Submission to God means that we confess our failures and our sins, and ask Him to work it out the right way. So, our first step to freedom and victory is submission to God!

Resist the Devil

The next step on the road to victory is to resist the devil. James 4:7 says, "Resist the devil and he will flee from you." Notice that the verse says to *resist* the devil—it doesn't say to play with him, engage in his games, mess with him or toy with his schemes. One might respond, "But, Pastor Steve, when do I play or flirt with the devil?" The fact of the matter is, we do this all the time. We mess around with the devil when we flirt with a married person at work. We mess around with the devil when we tell that little white lie to our spouse. A believer messes around with the devil when she starts dating an unbeliever. A person messes around with the devil when he gets too amorous with his girlfriend. We mess around with the devil when we decide to go to happy hour with the gang instead of heading home after work. These are just a few of the ways we give the devil a foothold.

Submitting to God means saying no to Satan. Therefore, even though I may want to do this particular thing, I'm going to refuse. Submitting means that even though I want to get angry, I'm going to love instead. It means that even though I want to tell you exactly what I'm thinking, I'm going to limit myself to words that build you up rather than tear you down. It means that even though I don't want to go home and work it out with my spouse, I'm choosing reconciliation. In other words, even though we may want to do what is wrong, we remember what Satan's trying to do, and we refuse to fall for it.

When we resist the devil, we are essentially saying, "Satan, you are not going to mess up my life. I'm not going to give you that room to work. I'm going to be faithful to God. I'm going to submit to Him and not play around with temptation."

The apostle Paul reminds believers, "'Be angry, and do not sin': do not let the sun go down on your wrath, nor give place to the devil" (Eph. 4:26-27). As Christians, we can "give place to the devil" when we flirt with temptation—when we have our little secret chamber and live a double standard. The moment we open the door to the devil, he puts his foot in, and the more we keep playing with sin, the more difficult it gets to close the door on him. It's far better to resist the devil and not give a place to him at all. But that requires waking up and understanding that those little temptations, if played with, become a stronghold for Satan.

It is common for people to be very ignorant when it comes to the wiles of the devil. As long as we have breath, we will always experience temptation. But here is where we often fail: We think of sin as being ugly, instead of realizing that the whole point of temptation is that sin can actually be fun and desirous for a season! Sometimes we get caught unaware when we are tempted and then feel horrified that we have been attracted to sin. As believers, we need to deal with the reality of temptation and then firmly choose not to feed our lusts.

In order to resist the devil and not give him a place to work in our lives, we need to stop flirting with temptation and sin. Remember, Jesus destroyed the work of the devil on the cross. The last thing we want to do as Christians is to resurrect the enemy's grasp on our lives.

I challenge each of us: We must walk out the Lord's victory over the enemy in our lives by resisting him and not giving him a place to do anything in our day-to-day life.

Draw Near to God

James continues, "Draw near to God and He will draw near to you" (v. 8). The third step toward freedom and victory is to draw near to God. Hebrews 10:22 says, "Let us draw near with a true heart in full assurance of faith, having our hearts sprinkled from an evil conscience and our bodies washed with pure water [the Word of God]."

As a pastor, I sometimes hear, "You don't know what I have done, Pastor Steve. I'm afraid to approach God." No matter what you have done, you can come before God with assurance. Enter the throne room and say, "God, I'm here. I need to get right with You. I need help." Don't crawl in with your tail between your legs. God says to come boldly before His throne (see Heb. 4:16). During Jesus' time on earth, everyone who came to Him was touched, healed and restored. Similarly, as long as a person has breath in his body, there is never a wrong time to run to God. Submitting to the Lord and drawing near to Him put us well on our way to victory.

Cleanse Your Hands

What is the most washed part of our bodies? Our hands. We cleanse them regularly to rid ourselves of germs that can harm us. So when James says to "cleanse your hands, you sinners" (v. 8), he communicates the fourth step to victory and freedom. The Lord wants us to cleanse ourselves from the things of this world, which are harmful, so that we can walk in close fellowship with Him. We must stop doing that which is wrong, put off the filth of the lust of the flesh, and put on the things of God. That is, we are to start doing the work of the Lord instead of the work of the flesh. Do you want victory in this life? I challenge you to "cleanse your hands" and keep yourself free from the stain of behaviors, thoughts and values that are characteristic of the world.

Purify Your Heart

James 4:8 goes on to share the fifth step to victory and freedom: "Purify your hearts, you double-minded."

Notice that being double-minded is connected to a problem with the heart. When our heart is not together, pure and whole, our mind is not together either. James tells us that we need to "purify our hearts," which means sin and fleshly lusts have been allowed to override our hearts for God. No longer is the Lord our first priority—we have allowed sin to defile our hearts. Is it any wonder that when we are in this situation, we are double-minded and unstable in all our ways? Godly choices and decisions are not forthcoming when our hearts are not right with God.

Do you want to stop the war within? Do you want to be overwhelmed by God's victory? If your answer is yes, then purify your heart; that is, repent and get right with God. The result will be an enjoyment of God's peace, no matter what circumstances you may be experiencing.

Mourn over Your Sins

Does our sin break our hearts? James exhorts us, "Lament and mourn and weep! Let your laughter be turned to mourning and your joy to gloom" (v. 9). Here we find the sixth step toward gaining victory and freedom.

I ask you, my dear reader, when was the last time you shed tears over your iniquity and sinfulness?

A condition for repentance is brokenness over our sin. Sometimes we are sorry that we got caught, so to speak, rather than being sorry for and broken over the actual sin. A true sign of repentance is genuine mourning over our sin. Now, it's not completely necessary to show outward emotional responses, though some certainly do. But there should be true grieving in our hearts over the sin we have committed. There may also be a sense of shame, regret, remorse, embarrassment and so on, but one thing is sure: We should have a mourning heart over the fact that we disobeyed God.

Why should our sin break our hearts? Because it was that sin that nailed our Lord to the cross. It was because of that sin that Jesus took a horrible beating. That truth should hurt and grieve us. Perhaps it would benefit us to watch the movie *The Passion of the Christ* every time we sin, just so we can be reminded how much it cost Jesus to take our sins upon Himself.

When we first become believers, we seem to be more sensitive to sin. We weep when we fail and are more cognizant of the pain of sin. That same mourning should continue to be present throughout our Christian lives, just as it was when we first received Christ. Mourning and grief over our sins should frequently exist. I am honestly troubled when leaders fall into sin and then show more concern for their lost position than for their sinfulness. God doesn't say to mourn over our loss of position or stature in the community; He definitely says to mourn over our sins. Truthfully, the Lord doesn't want us to "go through the motions" when we ask for forgiveness. His heart is for true repentance; He yearns for us to feel genuine grief over the things we have done that violate His standards—and to have an earnest desire to make things right.

Humble Yourself Before God

The seventh—and final—step to victory and freedom is to humble yourself before God. James communicates it well: "Humble yourselves in the sight of the Lord, and He will lift you up" (v. 10).

In the rest of the fourth chapter of his letter, James offers some practical applications of what it looks like for us to humble ourselves. First, humbling ourselves before God means loving others. As James puts it, "Do not speak evil of one another, brethren.

He who speaks evil of a brother and judges his brother, speaks evil of the law and judges the law. But if you judge the law, you are not a doer of the law but a judge. There is one Lawgiver, who is able to save and to destroy. Who are you to judge another?" (vv. 11-12). Because we are all sinners saved by grace, James makes it clear that we are not to judge our brothers and sisters in Christ or say anything evil about them. Only God can judge.

So, the first practical application of humbling ourselves before God is to love people, and Scripture gives us a specific picture of what this looks like. We don't speak evil of someone—we build up. We don't judge someone else—we look at the speck in our own eye instead. We don't bear a grudge against someone—we forgive.

Second, humbling ourselves before God means being willing to wait on Him. James tell us how to practically apply this concept: "Come now, you who say, 'Today or tomorrow we will go to such and such a city, spend a year there, buy and sell, and make a profit'; whereas you do not know what will happen tomorrow. For what is your life? It is even a vapor that appears for a little time and then vanishes away. Instead you ought to say, 'If the Lord wills, we shall live and do this or that'" (vv. 13-15).

If we are humble before God, we certainly are not going to tell Him what we will do. We are not going to grab for control over our lives and make plans without conferring with the Lord to see what His will is.

In fact, consider this: The problem that you are facing today just might have come about because you forged ahead and followed a path that you thought was the way to go, without considering what God wanted.

Being humble before God means that we give up control of our lives. It means that we are willing to wait on the Lord, to let Him guide us and then to obediently walk in His way instead of forging our own path. We don't "help" God out by trying to make something happen. God knows our hearts, and it's vital that we trust Him to take good care of us. When God calls the shots, we can't go wrong. And waiting on the Lord is proof that a believer is humble before God.

The final practical step of humbling ourselves before God is found in James 4:16-17, which reads, "But now you boast in your arrogance. All such boasting is evil. Therefore, to him who knows to do good and does not do it, to him it is sin."

James makes it clear that obedience to God is necessary, and that lack of obedience is sin. If a person says, "Well, I know I shouldn't do that," I respond with, "Then stop." He or she might retort, "Well, I just don't really feel convicted." Let's go back to verse 17: "To him who knows to do good and does not do it, to him it is sin." Lack of obedience is sin—and if we sin, what do we need to do? Humble ourselves.

Thanks to the apostle James, we have a clear picture of three practical ways to humble ourselves before God: love others, wait on God and be obedient to the Lord.

The war within will always be a part of our lives, to one degree or another, until the Lord takes us home. But we do not have to live in spiritual defeat. In fact, God wants us to walk in the Spirit, bear fruit, and live a victorious Christian life. If you are overwhelmed by spiritual defeat right now, take heart. God wants you to be over-whelmed with His victory. Consider the following story:

There was a pilot who, when flying one day, heard a gnawing noise in the fuselage of his plane. He was able to look and see that the culprit was a rat. The pilot knew that rodents are not able to withstand high altitudes, so he soared high in the sky—as high as he could go. After being up at that altitude for a number of minutes, he landed. Upon obser-vation, he saw that the rat was dead. The moral: The only way a Christian can defeat his enemy, Satan, is by rising spiritually in his Christian life.

Dear reader, I challenge you: Humble yourself and submit to God. Put Him first in your life and walk with Him on a daily basis, and you will experience the victory that God has in store for you rather than spiritual defeat.

STUDY QUESTIONS

1. How can we feed our spirit and not feed (fuel) our flesh?
2. What are the seven steps to freedom found in the book of James?
3. According to the apostle James, what are three practical ways we can humble ourselves before God?
4. What steps can you personally take right now to begin to gain victory over sin and temptation in your life?

∽ PRAYER ∽

Lord, I submit my life to You. I don't want to get caught up in the battle of sin or temptation; rather, I want victory. I want my spirit, not my flesh, to have control. Help me to flee temptation. Help me to say no to sin, and to run like the wind from the devil and not underestimate his tactics. Father, help me to trust You with all things in my life and to feed my spirit daily by Your Word. I do not want to grieve the Holy Spirit, and I desire victory in this battle of life. Help me to walk humbly before You every day. May Your will be done in and through my life today! Amen.

12

Overwhelmed by God's Promises . . .

instead of depression and anxiety

The promises of God are certain,
but they do not all mature in ninety days.
A. J. GORDON

For all the promises of God in Him are Yes,
and in Him Amen, to the glory of God through us.
2 CORINTHIANS 1:20

I recently read an interesting report. In 1994, a 67-year-old carpenter named Russell Herman died in Illinois. In his last will and testament, Mr. Herman left $2.4 billion to the town of Cave-In-Rock, $2.4 billion to the community of East St. Louis and $1.5 billion for projects in southeastern Illinois. That's pretty amazing—but there's more! In his final act of generosity, Mr. Herman also left $6 trillion to the Federal Reserve to pay off the national debt. There was only one problem: Mr. Herman only owned a 1983 Oldsmobile Toronado. Russell Herman may not have left behind anything of monetary value, but he did leave us all with a good reminder: We can't give what we don't possess. Mr. Herman's promises sounded great, but he did not have the resources to make them a reality. Fortunately, that is not the case with God. Our God has the means to make good on all His promises, and in a world of broken promises, it is good to know that God can be counted on.

Broken Promises

Have you ever thought about how many promises you have broken in your lifetime? The odds are that each of us has broken at least one promise to a spouse, a child or a friend—possibly all of the above. This kind of failure is inevitable for us because we are fallen people. Perhaps we think it's not a big deal, but it really is, because others need to be able to count on us—especially our spouse and our children.

Let's say you were to say to your wife, "Honey, I'd like to take you out for a cup of coffee tomorrow." It's important to realize that she is going to not only think about it, but also dream about it. That cup-of-coffee mini-date will have her thinking of you as her knight in shining armor—delivering a welcome break from the kids and a time of romance all wrapped around a cup of coffee. But let's say you wake up the next day feeling a little under the weather and decide to say to your wife, "I don't feel like getting a cup of coffee today." How will this decision impact your wife? She's going to be discouraged and cry or possibly be angry!

If this becomes a pattern, 20 years later, your wife is going to say to you, "You know, all you do is make promises and not keep them."

Seriously, breaking promises can have a devastating effect on people and relationships. If we let others down, especially on an ongoing basis, sooner or later they simply will not trust that we will deliver. We must be careful about what we promise. It's better not to promise anything than to make a commitment and then not keep our word. Bottom line, people are hurt when a promise is broken.

By the way, many people's current emotional problems stem from broken promises in the past: Parents, friends, a spouse or even the government promised something and never delivered. Hence, many people have a very difficult time trusting others. After all, if people don't keep their word, how can we trust anything they say?

As opposed to human beings, however, God never lies, and He will always keep His Word. We can bank on the fact that God will keep each and every promise He has ever made.

Are you overwhelmed by all the broken promises people have made? Perhaps your husband promised "'til death do us part," only to leave you and your children for someone else. Or maybe your dad spent many of your growing-up years promising that he would go to that "next" recital or sports event, only to let you down time and again.

This is my encouragement: Even though people often let us down, God never will. Therefore, we can absolutely trust the Lord to keep His promises to us. In addition, God will help us to forgive the people who have hurt us when we learn to let the pain of our lives rest in His hands. Because people are sinners, no matter how hard they try or how close they are to the Lord, there will never be a time when we don't experience some kind of disappointment at the hands of another person. But we can forgive people with grace because we trust God, and the Lord will uphold us with faithfulness even when others aren't faithful.

That being said, when it comes to keeping our own commitments, we need to do our utmost to be people who keep our word, even if it results in our own hurt or inconvenience. That's why God tells us to be careful with our words. We are responsible to think before we speak—to pray before we make a promise.

One day, when my daughter was young, she came to me asking if I would buy her a real horse. Touched by her heartfelt request, I told her to seek the Lord and ask Him because we simply couldn't afford one at the time. She walked away discouraged, tears dripping from her eyes. My heart sank, and I felt, for the first time, mad about being broke.

As months went by, my daughter seemed to have forgotten about the whole idea of having a real horse. Then one day my little girl plopped herself down in my office and asked me how my study was coming and whether she could get me anything. I knew that she was after something, so I asked her what I could do for her. She proceeded to tell me that someone had approached her at church the night before and asked her if it was true that she was interested in having a real horse. She answered yes, and the person told her that he had a horse he would give her for free.

My daughter started to jump up and down, so excited that God had answered her prayer and that she could have a horse for free. She asked me when we could pick it up, and I had to explain to her that our family had no place to put the horse and did not have the money to rent a stall and otherwise take care of such a large animal. My daughter just stared at me as if to say, "I can't believe that you, not only as my dad but also a pastor, would break your promise to me. You promised that if I prayed for a horse and God gave one to me, then I could have it!" Looking back, I could see that I really should have thought through the whole concept of owning a horse when the subject first came up. Instead, I broke my daughter's heart by breaking a promise. It was a tough lesson learned.

God wants us to walk closely with Him on a daily basis so that He can help us in our commitments, relationships and promises. But even when we fail other people, the Lord is faithful to us. He is going to keep every one of His promises to us and bring us to Himself.

Now, just in case you think God's promises are not for you, or that His promises are only for "perfect" people, I want to show you otherwise by taking a look at a man named Jacob.

The Story of Jacob

Each of us has been overwhelmed at some point—perhaps at many points—in our lives. Whenever we find ourselves in one of those difficult seasons, we have to remember that the promises of God are our strength and our encouragement to keep going when the journey gets rough. These promises are an amazing gift from a gracious God. Let's look at the story of Jacob and discover how God made great promises to this less-than-worthy man with affirmations of His presence and commitment. There are certainly applications we can make to our own journey as well.

Jacob was the son of the well-known patriarch, Isaac, and Isaac's wife, Rebekah. Jacob also had a twin brother, Esau. Let's begin to examine this family's story at the point when Isaac was old and blind. Isaac summoned Esau, who was the elder brother, and said, "Behold now, I am old. I do not know the day of my death. Now therefore, please take your weapons, your quiver and your bow, and go out to the field and hunt game for me. And make me savory food, such as I love, and bring it to me that I may eat, that my soul may bless you before I die" (Gen. 27:2-4).

Isaac's plan was to give Esau his blessing. In that day, the first-born male child of a family would typically receive an extra inheritance upon his father's death. The eldest son would get one-half of the estate, and the other children would divide equally the other portion of the estate. So Isaac sent for his firstborn son, Esau, in order to bestow this final blessing on him. He also asked his son to kill a deer, so he could eat his favorite meal of venison one more time.

Rebekah overheard her husband calling for Esau, and she sent for Jacob while Esau was out in the fields hunting. Even though Jacob was about 30 years old at this point, he was still a mama's boy, so to speak. Rebekah wanted Jacob to receive the blessing instead of Esau, so she devised a deceptive plan.

Rebekah said, in essence, "Listen, Jacob, your father is going to give away the blessing. This is what we are going to do. I am going to go out and kill an animal, cut it up, and wrap it around your arms so that when he touches your arm, he will feel the hair and think it is Esau. Your father is going to smell you, too, so we are going to put some dirt and blood on you so that you smell like Esau."

Rebekah then fixed a nice dinner of venison and said, "Here, Jacob, take this in to your father."

Jacob took the meal in to Isaac and said, "Father, I was able to catch the game." Isaac was surprised at how quickly it seemed Esau had found the game. Jacob lied to his father, basically saying, "Well, God was with me. I caught it quickly."

Isaac's well-founded confusion continued: "Please come near, that I may feel you, my son. . . . The voice is Jacob's voice, but the hands are the hands of Esau" (Gen. 27:21-22). Jacob continued to deceive and lie to his father until Isaac prayed over Jacob—and the blessing came upon Jacob instead of Esau.

When Esau found out what had happened, he was naturally livid and intended to kill Jacob. Jacob fled for his life, running toward Laban, Rebekah's brother, in Haran. Although Jacob was known as a conniver, he felt guilty and ashamed about what he had done. Not only that, but he was also tired, exhausted and overwhelmed. As he was running, he came to the Syrian Desert and found a place to sleep, because it was getting dark. The Bible says that he grabbed a rock and used it as a pillow (see Gen. 28:11). Jacob went to sleep with his head lying on that rock. That's when God intervened in the life of Jacob and made incredible promises to him—promises that extend to us today as well.

God's Promises

God spoke to Jacob in a dream. Genesis 28:15 records the Lord's words: "Behold, I am with you and will keep you wherever you go, and will bring you back to this land; for I will not leave you until I have done what I have spoken to you."

In verse 16, we read Jacob's response: "Then Jacob awoke from his sleep and said, 'Surely the Lord is in this place, and I did not know it.'"

The Lord unmistakably communicated to Jacob who He was, how He would bless Jacob and that He would never leave him. These amazing promises of God are for us as well. It is common to feel like the Lord is not with us; in fact, that is often our human way of thinking. We don't realize that God is with us on the freeway or at our workplace, but He is right there. We don't acknowledge that God is with us when it comes time to talk to the kids or our spouse, but He is right there.

After God spoke to Jacob in that dream, Jacob realized that the Lord was in the place where he was, but he had not recognized that before. Because we are believers in Christ, the Lord has made a covenant with us never to leave us or forsake us (see Deut. 31:6). He has also promised to finish the work He has begun in us (see Phil. 1:6). The journey might get complex and thorny, but the promises of God remain absolute and steadfast.

Some of us likely feel as if we do not deserve God's promises. Perhaps that guilt stems from an ongoing struggle with a nagging sin, an apathy toward our relationship with the Lord, or a greater desire for the world and its trappings than for spiritual things. Well, Jacob didn't deserve God's favor either. Here was a man who was a conniver and a deceiver—it was a way of life for him. Jacob stole Esau's birthright in exchange for a bowl of stew (see Gen. 25:29-34). Then he conspired with his mother to deceive his own father—stealing the firstborn blessing from Esau. But in spite of all that, God indicated, "This is the man I want to bless and use to help My people."

Just as He chose Jacob, God has also chosen us. God wants a close relationship with us and wants us to walk with Him on a daily basis. He is keenly aware that we humans are not perfect, "for He knows our frame; He remembers that we are dust" (Ps. 103:14). Even when we are faithless, our Lord is faithful to us (see 2 Tim. 2:13). Bottom line, we sin, we fail our families, we get divorced, we lie and deceive—truly, the list of our depravity is long. Even so, the Lord is going to pick us up and never cease to be with us in the midst of any painful situation—whether one we cause by our own sin or one that is inflicted upon us. He wants relationship with His children so that His perfect will can be done in our lives. Even when we blow it—when we sin, fall down and fail—the Lord faithfully keeps every one of His promises to us.

Therefore, no matter what circumstances we find ourselves in right now, we should cling to the encouragement and comfort that God is with us. He will never forsake us, and He has given us His many promises. Let's take a closer look at three very important promises that He gave to Jacob—because they also extend their life-giving grace and blessing to each of us.

"I Am with You"

Let's reread Genesis 28:15: "Behold, I am with you and will keep you wherever you go, and will bring you back to this land; for I will not leave you until I have done what I have spoken to you."

The first promise we'll examine is: "Behold, I am with you." That's downright awesome, don't you think? The fact that God is with us should encourage our hearts, especially when we are overwhelmed by trials and problems. That means, when we are righteous, pure and holy, God is with us. That also means, however, that when we have backslidden and made mistakes, God is with us. Finally, even when we are nasty and mean toward others or angry toward God, He is still with us. We undoubtedly can be unstable and sway with the wind, but God is constant in His promise, and His faithfulness toward us never changes.

If we truly fathomed the reality that God is with us at every moment, we would think and act much differently. Like Jacob, who said, "Surely the Lord is in this place, and I did not know it" (Gen. 28:16), we, too, can be unaware of His presence—and act like we think He is nowhere nearby. I felt that way during the early part of my time in the hospital. I just didn't feel like the Lord was with me in that hospital room. He was, of course, and if I had recognized that truth sooner, no doubt my hospital stay would have been much more peaceful, encouraging and uplifting to others.

The author of Hebrews says, "Let your conduct [or better yet, translated directly from the Greek, 'your manner of life'] be without covetousness; be content with such things as you have. For He Himself has said, 'I will never leave you nor forsake you'" (Heb. 13:5). The verse is crystal clear. Will God leave us? Never. Will God forsake us? Never. We belong to Him.

As I mentioned earlier, sometimes we mistakenly assume that God is not with us because we have backslidden, are sinning or are not walking closely with Him. Yet, even in our backslidden state, God is still with us. The Lord has not left us, even if we have fallen away. However, once again enjoying His fellowship requires that we repent and reconnect with Him.

The apostle Peter laid out this principle: "Repent therefore and be converted, that your sins may be blotted out, so that times of refreshing may come from the presence of the Lord" (Acts 3:19). It's critical that we pay close attention to this. When we have backslidden or fallen away from the Lord, it's unnecessary to be saved again or to bring Jesus back into our hearts—because He never left us. What we do have to do is "repent therefore" so that "times of refreshing may come." Just like when our computer stalls, we sometimes need to hit the "refresh" button to get our relationship with God back on the right track.

Let me reiterate: Any idea that we have to be resaved is wrong. All we need to do, at any moment, is call on God's never-ending mercy and His constant presence with these words: "God, forgive me. Please, make Yourself known to me. Help me understand that You are here. God, You gave me a promise: You are never going to leave me or forsake me." Then we must believe in faith that He has heard and forgiven—and walk forward in confidence and with transformed actions.

The apostle Paul, while preaching to people in Athens, communicated the truth that, although God is great and "not served by human hands," He also is always surrounding us and calling us to seek Him. Paul declared, "From one man he made all the nations, that they should inhabit the whole earth; and he marked out their appointed times in history and the boundaries of their lands. God did this so that they would seek him and perhaps reach out for him and find him, though he is not far from any one of us. 'For in him we live and move and have our being'" (Acts 17:25-28, *NIV*).

So we live, we move, and we have our being in the presence of God. That means, when Jacob was in the tent deceiving Isaac, God was there with him. When Jacob fled down that dusty road from his brother, Esau, God traveled alongside him. When Jacob went to sleep in the desert, God was still with him. And while Jacob was sleeping, God woke him up, so to speak. Jacob realized something was different when God gave him that dream. What did Jacob discover? That God was there. This truth is vitally important for us to realize as well. Allowing our feelings of being overwhelmed, lonely or in despair to bring us down must be battled, because God has promised that He is with us and will never leave us or forsake us.

"I Will Keep You"

Genesis 28:15 also contains the second promise of God to Jacob— and to us. God says, "I . . . will keep you wherever you go."

He will keep us wherever we go. In other words, because we are God's children, He promises to make sure we finish the race. First Peter 1:5 relays that Peter is writing to believers—to those "who are kept by the power of God." A lifelong walk of faith is too much for us to handle without God's power. Our job is to fix our eyes on Jesus, and the Lord's job is to keep us in the faith until the end.

One New Testament writer, Jude, refers to God as "Him who is able to keep you from stumbling, and to present you faultless before the presence of His glory with exceeding joy" (Jude 1:24). The Lord will keep us from walking out or quitting. We struggle, it seems, to realize just how much God wants to help us. He doesn't leave things in our hands. We've all heard people sigh and complain, "It seems like everything is up to me." But that is the enemy's lie to us as believers. God promises not only to be with us at every moment for the rest of our lives, but also to keep us in the faith until the end. His keeping power can stop us from going down the path of destruction; it can hold marriages together. Bottom line, He alone can protect lives from falling apart.

The apostle Paul, who put his very existence into the hands of this promise-keeping God, eloquently wrote, "For this reason I also suffer these things; nevertheless I am not ashamed, for I know whom I have believed and am persuaded that He is able to keep what I have committed to Him until that Day" (2 Tim. 1:12). If we have given God our heart and our life, then He has promised to keep them. What we give God, we are never going to lose.

Would you agree that nothing is too hard for God? The prophet Jeremiah was convinced of that truth, exalting God's greatness with these words: "Ah, Lord God! Behold, You have made the heavens and the earth by Your great power and outstretched arm. There is nothing too hard for You" (Jer. 32:17). With that in mind, do we really think that the problem we are currently overwhelmed by is too much for God to handle? Can He not accomplish His perfect and good will in us through this problem? The enemy would like for us to believe the lie that our situation is hopeless, but it's not too hard for God to find a job, to heal a marriage or to bring back prodigal children. Whatever problems or trials we are facing today, it's critical to believe in faith that God is able to fix them and even work through them to bring about His good and perfect will.

Notice the last part of Genesis 28:15: "for I will not leave you until I have done what I have spoken to you." This part of the promise should produce wonderful relief. God finishes what He starts. He's not going to leave anything undone in our lives. That means, the work He is doing in our marriage, He is going to continue until He is done. The work He is doing in our hearts, He is going to bring to completion. God's keeping power will keep us walking in His way until He takes us home to live forever with Him. That's a promise we can take to the bank!

"I Will Make You"
What did Jesus say to the men who would become His disciples? "Follow Me, and I will make you fishers of men" (Matt. 4:19).

God promises to make, mold and transform us into the people He wants us to be. He will hone our gifts and strengths and exercise our personality, not only to bring other people to Him, but also to make us the best we can be. We can without doubt be "confident of this very thing, that He who has begun a good work in [us] will complete it until the day of Jesus Christ" (Phil. 1:6). Therefore, as Paul assures us in this affirmation of God's promises, the Lord will make us a better businessman, a better husband, a better dad, a better mom, a better wife, a better pastor, a better disciple, a better student and a better friend. God is going to build each of us into a holy person who reflects His glory and character.

One key method the Lord uses in transforming us into better people is working through the trials He allows in our lives. The Lord uses these trials and problems to mold us into His image. He will not leave us as the people we are now, but is faithful to complete His good work. Like an artist perfecting his masterpiece, God is chiseling us into a beautiful mirrored image of Jesus Christ. He wants others to see His reflection when they look at us, watch our behaviors, and hear us speak. Only God has the wisdom and perfect plan to shape us into the people He wants us to be; He alone has the patience, the power and the stick-to-itiveness to complete the task.

God's promises are real. He will never break them. We can count on His utter faithfulness to fulfill His promises; when we make this choice of faith and trust, we will find that we are overwhelmed by God instead of our problems. It bears repeating: God will never leave us or forsake us. In summary, let's revisit the immeasurable promises of God. First, God says, "I am with you." This promise banishes loneliness as a reality. Second, He says, "I will keep you." He will keep us in what we are doing, from what we are doing, away from the enemy and the enemy away from us.

Finally, God will make us—building into us, producing character in us and making us better people. Just as Jacob received the promises of God for his life, so too can we. Let's soak in and be grateful for this promise: "The Lord your God, He is God, the faithful God who keeps covenant and mercy for a thousand generations with those who love Him and keep His commandments" (Deut. 7:9). I'm grateful for our promise-keeping God; are you?

STUDY QUESTIONS

1. God has promised to finish the work He has begun in us. What are the three important promises that God gave to Jacob and to us?
2. What does God mean when He promises us, "I am with you"?
3. What does God mean when He promises us, "I will keep you"?
4. What does God mean when He promises us, "I will make you"?

∽ PRAYER ∽

Lord, thank You that You overwhelm my life with Your promises and Your presence. I know that Your hand is upon every aspect of my life, and that Your plans for me are good to an expected end. Thank You that You will not leave me in the state I am in, but that You have a purpose and a calling for me, and that You are committed to completing Your work in me. Put my eyes back upon You, I pray. Strengthen me with Your power and help me to bear fruit in all that I do. I want to shine for Your glory and not be pressed down by my circumstances and feelings. Help me to stand upon Your promises and faithful presence today and in the days ahead. Refresh me, encourage me and be the lifter of my head. Fill me with Your peace and let me be overwhelmed by You, I pray. Amen.

Epilogue

Once Overwhelmed, but God . . .

my story

When you say a situation or a person is hopeless,
you are slamming the door in the face of God.
A. J. GORDON

For I know the thoughts that I think toward you, says the LORD,
thoughts of peace and not of evil, to give you a future and a hope.
JEREMIAH 29:11

In various seasons of my life, I definitely have felt overwhelmed—never more so than following an event that took place during my younger years. Even though I was blessed early on with a wholesome family life and a healthy upbringing, one day everything changed. Afterward, I fervently wished that that day would somehow go away forever; instead, it left a powerfully devastating impact, forcing my life into a downward spiral of anger, guilt and horrible shame. That was the day my innocence was taken from me forever.

This traumatic event was a turning point for me; I came home from school that day a changed person. The light went out from my life. My eyes darkened; my behavior became hostile. Yet no one could figure out what had happened to me, because I remained silent.

On that day, a respected authority figure—a schoolteacher—sexually molested me. The teacher lured me off campus by promising me extra credit for helping him with a project. As soon as we were distanced from the school, the teacher told me to take my clothes off. I knew I was in danger. I was even more horrified when the teacher took out a camera. Afraid that the teacher would harm me, I complied with what he wanted me to do. I remember crying out in my heart, wanting the whole situation to go away.

Have you ever been overwhelmed by a traumatic event in your life? Have you ever cried out in your heart, just wanting the whole situation to disappear? I understand how you feel.

I would like to say that I turned to God in the days following that moment, but I didn't. Instead, I was full of hatred and bitterness. No matter how hard I tried to forget and to run from the horrible trauma I had experienced, I couldn't escape the pain and shame that I carried in my heart. Instead of turning to God for help, I turned to drugs and eventually to a Harley-Davidson motorcycle gang.

Soon my life was spinning out of control. Guns, violence, crime and drugs became my norm. I was shot, I was arrested and I was wanted by the FBI for a short time. Eventually, even the motorcycle gang evicted me from their home. I started sleeping in gutters and became a homeless man. But God had a miraculous plan for me.

One day, a husband and wife named Henry and Shirley discovered me as they came out to their car, which was parked near the gutter in which I was sleeping. Amazingly, they invited me into their home, allowed me to take a long-overdue shower, and fed me a meal. Shirley had a vision of hope for me and told me that she saw Jesus in my eyes. She and Henry had been on their way to church and invited me to go with them, which, surprisingly, I did.

The church they took me to was very different from the church I had attended as a child. There were swarms of young people—hippies just like me with long hair, bell-bottoms and bare feet.

The church was packed; many people stood around the edges, and some even sat on the floor. This place was different. I noticed businessmen in their suits embracing the hippies. I found myself thinking, *What could these people possibly have in common?* Everyone was hugging, and they all had huge smiles on their faces. I felt compelled to be a part of whatever was happening in that place.

When the pastor, Chuck Smith, came out to greet everyone, he wasn't at all what I expected. I listened intently and, for the first time in years, was intrigued by this "authority figure." He seemed different from typical preachers. His huge smile just captivated me, and I saw in him a man I could admire. Pastor Chuck possessed a strength that I had never seen before. He was built like a rock, and he spoke like a prophet of God. Genuine love radiated from his eyes. This man was different, and right then, I knew I wanted whatever it was that he had. Each word Pastor Chuck spoke cut to my heart.

At the end of the service, Pastor Chuck gave an invitation. Anyone who wanted to receive Jesus Christ as his or her Lord and personal Savior was called to go forward to the front of the church for prayer. I instinctively knew that this was what I needed. It was so different from anything I had tried before. I somehow comprehended that the love I was experiencing that night was supernatural; it could only be God. God was calling me and drawing me out of Satan's grip into His loving arms.

That very night, I accepted the salvation of Jesus Christ, and that was the beginning of my new life—a life no longer overwhelmed by trauma, anger, shame, bitterness, paranoia, drugs and darkness. Even though on the surface I had looked like a hopeless case, because of God, I was not. Guess what? Neither are you! Have people given up on you? More to the point, have you given up on yourself? Are you so overwhelmed by hurt, pain, trauma and loss that all seems hopeless in your life? My life is a testimony that no matter how badly things may unravel, God is always there for you, and with Him, nothing is impossible—absolutely nothing!

Walking with the Lord is a lifelong process. Forty years have passed since I accepted the Lord. As the Potter, God has done His work of shaping me and using me for His glory in ways that are hard to believe, considering where I was when He drew me to Himself. Even so, over the years, there have been multiple times when I was overwhelmed, choosing to focus on the problems in my life rather than keep my eyes on the Lord.

Early on in ministry, for example, plagued by self-doubt and insecurity, I quit as senior pastor of a church I had started. I left the senior pastor role in order to be an assistant pastor elsewhere—a much safer choice for me, or so I thought. Then I received a call from Pastor Chuck, who asked, "Steve, why am I the last one to find out about you leaving your church?" Chuck proceeded to tell me that a true shepherd never shocks the people; rather, he warns them. Chuck lovingly chastened me about leaving my church the way I did. He finished the call with these last words: "Steve, you are not a shepherd. Next time, call me first!"

I was devastated beyond belief and totally overwhelmed by my failure. It was like God Himself had spoken to me over the phone, chastening me for my foolishness and immaturity. Even so, amid all my tears, shame and anguish, two words stood out like towers of hope. The Holy Spirit must have shouted them into my heart. The two words were: "Next time." I thought to myself, *Yes, that is what Pastor Chuck said: "Next time."* Then I remember thinking, *God, could there ever be a next time?* The voice of condemnation rang loudly in my head, thanks to Satan, the enemy of our souls. How could there be a next time when everything I did seemed to end in failure? How could anyone ever trust me again? I kept pondering, *God, could there ever be a next time?* My heart's prayer was: "Forgive me, Lord, for my foolishness, and if I have hurt anyone, please help them in their personal walk with You."

Stunningly, by His grace, God was not finished with me. Little did I know that I was really just starting to go down this path of ministry.

A few years went by, during which I tried to give up the thought of ever being a senior pastor of a church. I was unsuccessful. In fact, I grew so impatient that I took matters into my own hands. I began writing out my ministry résumé. I listed my accomplishments and named the churches where I had been a pastor. Why? I believe my heart was hungry for ministry, and I couldn't let go of the possibility of shepherding a church again—in fact, I was getting excited about it.

One day, I wrote letters to a number of friends and colleagues who might be able to find me a church to pastor; I was so excited, I could hardly wait to get to the post office. At that moment, as clear as day, the Holy Spirit spoke to me: "Where do you think you're going with those letters?" I froze in my tracks. The few seconds before He spoke again felt like hours. I heard the Spirit's words; they burned within my heart: "Stephen, I thought we made a covenant that you would wait on Me—and that when the time was right, I would speak to Pastor Chuck, and he would call you."

The words burned with conviction, and I felt emptiness deep inside. Why emptiness? Because I realized that what I said and believed were not the same as how I acted, and the Holy Spirit knew it. Truly my heart was right, but my patience was zero. I was doing what we all do so often—trying to help out the Holy Spirit. Once again the eyes of my heart were opened, and I was reminded that the Holy Spirit does not need my help. That day, I was overwhelmed by my wicked heart. I wept when my wife, Gail, looked at me and said, "Not again!" This was the real problem in my life. I struggled to be patient and wait for God's timing.

Earlier in my life, the Lord had begun to teach me this lesson, but I am a hard-headed student. At the end of one school year in high school, one of my favorite teachers maintained the tradition of giving each student something to help us remember her class. She gave everyone in the class a small trophy, except for me. Instead, she gave me a rock—an ugly, petrified rock. I remember being ridiculed and mocked by the other students. Yet the teacher stood in front of my desk and said, "Stephen, I am giving you this rock because you have no patience at all. It took thousands of years to make this a petrified rock, and it will take years for you to find out what God is doing in your life."

I received her message—in fact, God's message—loud and clear, despite the fact that I was terrified about what to tell my parents, knowing they would not be pleased that every student except me had received a trophy. In my fear, I lied and told my dad that the rock was the first-place prize for the class. He told me that he was proud of me, and my mom placed the rock on the mantle to be seen by everyone.

I hated that rock and was embarrassed and ashamed every time I thought of it over the years. But on the day of the Holy Spirit's conviction, my teacher's words returned to challenge me: "Stephen, in patience you will find your greatness; just be patient with yourself and everything will work out." The Holy Spirit then reminded me of my final stipulation to the Lord—that Chuck Smith was going to have to personally call me with a position.

At a place of desperation and brokenness, I finally let go and gave up the dream. Then, sometime later, while on a long-overdue vacation, I started to talk to the Lord again about being a senior pastor. I asked Him for a sign: "If I am ever going to pastor again, Lord, please let me catch a fish before this hook leaves the water." After fishing for about an hour, I started to reel in my line, because my wife and kids were in the car waiting for me. As the hook got close to the surface and was about to break the top of the water, my eyes welled up with tears. No fish would bite now; it was too late. But just as the hook was coming out of the water, a tiny fish bit it. I brought the fish closer, where I could get my hands on it; it was so small that I unhooked it and released it back into the lake. Even so, that tiny fish meant more to me than any five-pound bass. I knew God had heard my cry and given me a sign.

After coming home from my vacation, I got a message that I was to call Pastor Chuck. When I returned his call, he told me that I had been unanimously selected to be the new senior pastor of Calvary Chapel South Bay in Los Angeles. In 1980, I walked into my new church, which at the time had about 50 members. Now, 33 years later, Calvary Chapel South Bay is home to about 9,000 people. God used my overwhelming failures to teach me to be faithful in the small things, to patiently wait on His timing, to be humble and to be a shepherd to the people whom He would eventually put in my charge.

I want to ask you: Are you overwhelmed by the failures in your life? Perhaps you are nursing a wound from a failed marriage, or you are heartbroken and filled with guilt over the direction your children have taken. Maybe your business has gone bankrupt or you have lost a house to foreclosure.

God is keenly aware of all the disappointments and failures we have experienced. Miraculously, He is able and willing to use those failures to bring us to the place He desires us to be—a place of faith and hope. There is always hope. There is always another chance, because God never gives up and never stops loving us. He is faithful even when we are not.

A third area in my life that has often been overwhelming, as I have shared earlier in this book, is my continuing poor physical health. My struggles have included cancer; chronic fatigue syndrome; sleep apnea; numerous surgeries to fix my gall bladder, nose, pancreas, shoulders, hips, back and knees; and finally knee replacements! My recent tragic back situation resulted in titanium rods being placed throughout my spine from vertebrae L1 to T10. Whether it is the immense pain I've suffered through all my ailments and surgeries or the time I've spent in hospitals or at home recuperating, dealing with these health problems has been immensely overwhelming.

On more than one occasion, I have asked God, "Why?"

The Lord has replied, "Why not, Steve?"

Although I will never fully fathom all of God's reasons for allowing poor health in my life, I do know that He has used this hardship to humble me and to help me realize that He is far more interested in working in me and my character than He is in healing me. You may recall that the most recent surgeries on my back had me out of the pulpit for nearly eight months. That is a really long time. Yet through all of that, my church prospered. This was a definite lesson to me that the Lord doesn't need Steve Mays, but Steve Mays needs the Lord!

I would imagine that there are some readers of this book who suffer with poor health as I do. Are you overwhelmed by cancer? Are you overwhelmed by physical pain that keeps you awake at night? Perhaps you are just plain weary of being sick and not feeling well. Allow God to overwhelm you with His compassion and love. Let God do His work. He has a divine purpose and uses everything—yes, everything—for your good. The sickness, the cancer, the disease, the broken parts of your body—even in all of that, the Lord is at work. Instead of asking, "Why?" I encourage you to ask the Lord, "What do You want to do in me and through me during this season of health struggles?"

As I wrote this last chapter, it was my goal to use it to give you a sampling of the issues and seasons in my own life that have been or continue to be overwhelming. To be sure, there are many more. In fact, if you are interested in reading further about my story, feel free to email or call Calvary Chapel South Bay and ask for the booklet titled *A Heart Beat from Hell: A Choice for Life,* which details my life story.

I understand what it feels like to be overwhelmed—I really do. But no matter what situations or trials you are walking through right now, I want to assure you that God is completely aware, He is sovereign and in control, and He will use the situations to do a mighty work *in* you and *through* you. May I share my best advice?

Stop fighting the Lord and let Him do His work. Allow yourself to be overwhelmed by . . .

His love . . .

His grace . . .

His forgiveness . . .

His mercy . . .

His purpose . . .

His power . . .

His holiness . . .

His Spirit . . .

His Word . . .

His provision . . .

His victory . . .

And His promises . . .

Reach out to the Lord your God. He desires to lift the burden from your shoulders and carry it for you. Isn't that what He makes clear in the Scriptures? "Cast your cares on the LORD and he will sustain you; he will never let the righteous be shaken" (Ps. 55:22). You—and all your struggles—matter to Him. Perhaps things are so tough right now that you don't even care about yourself anymore, but God still lovingly and faithfully cares about you. He yearns for you to love Him greatly and trust Him wholeheartedly with your life.

I recently told my congregation, "I may have a broken body, but my spirit is not broken!" They responded with applause and gave praise to God. With tears in my eyes, I had to admit for the first time that I now have physical limitations in my life. However, thanks to the Lord, I am still able to preach and move people's hearts toward the kingdom of God. What a blessing that He would do that through me!

I challenge you to meditate on this question: *Are you willing to choose to be overwhelmed by God instead of by your troubles so that you may live in peace and with abundant joy?* I pray, my dear reader, that your answer is yes.

∽ PRAYER ∽

Lord, open the eyes of Your people to Your overwhelming power—power that is available to us when we stop and allow You to intervene in and through our lives. Change our perspective, Lord, so that we see Your hand upon every area of our lives—not just focusing on our trials. Help us to view our challenges and painful circumstances as opportunities to turn to You, to be overwhelmed by You and to give You glory. Work in us and through us, and have Your way in our lives, we pray. We surrender to You, Lord. Amen.

ALSO BY
Steve Mays

A Heartbeat from Hell

Un Latido del Infierno

Choices

Crossing the Line

VICTORY IS YOURS TO WIN!

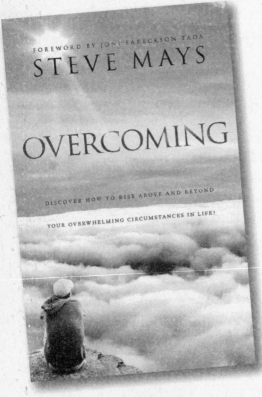

OVERCOMING
Steve Mays
ISBN: 978.08307.62002

Bad things can (and do) happen to good people. Sometimes difficult circumstances are the natural result of our own choices, but other times they stem from someone else's bad behavior. Whatever your situation, God is calling you to move beyond adversity and live a victorious life that brings glory to His name.

Can you overcome your debilitating emotions? Pastor Steve Mays insists that you can, by the power of the Holy Spirit. In *Overcoming*, you'll find solid, biblical guidance for winning the victory over circumstances that threaten to derail your wholehearted pursuit of God.

Are you ready to rise above?